AF522373

My Life
The Journey of a Dalit Sociologist

My Life
The Journey of a Dalit Sociologist

Govardhan Wankhede

My Life: The Journey of a Dalit Sociologist
Govardhan Wankhede

© Author

First Published 2020

ISBN 978-93-5002-685-4

All rights reserved. No part of this book may be reproduced or transmitted, in any form or by any means, without the prior permission of the Publisher.

Published by
AAKAR BOOKS
28 E Pocket IV, Mayur Vihar Phase I
Delhi 110 091 India
aakarbooks@gmail.com

Laser Typeset at
Arpit Printographers, Delhi

Printed at
Sapra Brothers, Noida.

I dedicate this life story to all those struggling for social emancipation and self-respect.

Contents

Acknowledgements

As many writers would agree, it is a great sense of happiness, achievement and relief that I feel to have finally completed telling my life story in the following pages. It took me more than two years to complete the manuscript owing to many official and personal preoccupations causing several gaps and pauses. Most importantly, revisiting my childhood and village-life and the accompanying social conditions made me acutely aware of difficulties I faced which caused several sleepless nights. Very often I would be overwhelmed and in tears while recalling my experiences of poverty, caste discrimination, untouchability and the life conditions of other members of my community. The transition from the painfully complex difficulties of the often-romanticized village life of my past to the present is quite unbelievable and the two seem so unrelated.

I cannot help but acknowledge that such social conditions and exploitation exist all over the world in the name of God or religion or both. The forms vary under titles of race, ethnicity, religion, tribe and gender. In India, caste and untouchability were created and approved in the name of God and religion sanctioning such barbaric and inhuman treatment of humans by humans. At the same time one can trace a long history of the struggle to overcome such a large-scale suppression of the majority by the minority. This, in the Indian context, is often mistaken for the rivalry between the rich and the poor, whereas the truth runs much deeper.

At the same time in India, which is inherently based on inequality and exploitation, there has been a long history of the efforts made by different stalwarts to liberate the oppressed. The advent of the British education system has been the beginning of such efforts in modern India. Education has been seen as one of the important means for such liberation, encouraged and agreed upon by the great reformers such as Jyotiba Phule, Dr. B.R. Ambedkar and many others who came into contact with Western education.

We are close to celebrating the platinum jubilee of our freedom, the freedom that can be viewed as a flow of the clash between national and human values. One can at least argue over the faith and practice of human values in a free and democratic India. It is pertinent to always remember one's own responsibilities towards these values, however difficult and challenging.

I have always tried to look at the world from a perspective which has evolved from the real experiences of my life—from caste, untouchability, poverty, discrimination and all kinds of humiliations that created my distinct perspective, firstly, as a member of Indian society, secondly as a citizen of this country and finally, as a trained sociologist. Ultimately, what are our gains and what are the losses and what direction we are moving in the areas of social change—from past, to the present and to the future—are matters of serious concern. In this context, one needs serious and honest answers to 'what', 'why', 'how' and 'by whom'. However, 'hope' is the constant source of dignity and a successful life.

I must mention here that several persons, friends, my professors, colleagues and well-wishers have been encouraging and insisting that I should write my life story.

I am grateful for their encouraging support that has finally materialized.

I am personally indebted to my parents and brothers who always encouraged me and extended active support to complete my PhD without pressure to discontinue my education and follow an economic pursuit.

My better half Radha, son Vikrant and daughter Shweta always supported and motivated me to write this story. I am thankful to them. Shweta and Vikrant have been confident enough to give their comments and correct the language— second generation benefit (?)—till the final draft of the manuscript. My special thanks to both of them.

I am aware of the fact that some educated Dalit friends are not in favour of writing such personal experiences of life and make it a public exhibition. I respect their views with great humility. My view is that unless you speak and write, people will not know and empathize and in that case you are missing and losing the social and academic values of such writings that will be conspicuously missing from the history of a society. It is important to write for our coming generations as well, as they inhabit a different and ever-changing world.

A special mention is a must to express my sincere gratitude to Anusha Ramnathan and Gauri Keshavan for their comments and suggestions to complete this work.

Lastly, I attribute my every success and achievement to Dr. Babasaheb Bhimrao Ambedkar, the saviour of all the downtrodden, who has been the constant source of inspiration for me. I bow my head before him, his genius and salute his undeniable contributions towards Indian society and Indians.

April 2020 **Govardhan Wankhede**
Navi Mumbai

1

Contextualizing the Life Story

Social change is the essential characteristic of any society. However, the change is dependent on two forces; first, the external and second, the internal, both affecting each other, positively or negatively. Both types depend on societal structure: rigidity and openness and its social institutions of which the individual is the member. Individuals contribute to the society in many ways but within given norms and rules. The relationship between the individual and society is guided by formal and informal relations. However an individual is born in the institution (family) first and then becomes the member of society. Society then is seen to be never static. In other words, we can call it, both individual and society run on the basic social facts that are inter-dependent, inter-linked and are inter-connected. For example, in Indian society, an individual is born in a family first and then he/she becomes a member of a community, caste and religion, culture, education, economy, etc depending on the position of the social layer of each institution that has inherent attributions of high-low, pure-impure, rich-poor ultimately resulting into gains and losses, deprivation and discrimination with a wide distance and hierarchy between individuals. Indian society could be the best example of this distance and gap or hierarchy due to its close, complex and rigid nature where an individual is strictly bound by several institutions such as family, caste, community and religion which have social and religious sanction. Owing to such a situation, most of the communities in Indian society got deprived socio-economically and culturally.

The Dalits (SCs), former untouchables, forming a significant part of the population, thus, have been deprived in many ways and became the victim of untouchability and poverty, indignity and discrimination for centuries with social and religious sanction. However, due to external modern forces of change like industrialization, colonial rule, modern education, Indian society was forced to adopt and adapt to these changes along with modern values like humanity, equality and social justice followed by independence and adoption of the democratic form of governance. However, one cannot say that these modern forces brought complete change but sowed the seeds of change. The agents of change, however, reached these communities too late and formal efforts made to bring the change in their lives have proved half way. Hence we see the social fabric in the form of "continuity and change."

In the given context, it will be worth knowing the lived and direct experiences of an individual coming from the lowest rank of society. The victim of all the social practices with immensely poor conditions and his struggle for education and search for new social identity will be worth reading and yet found to be in a fix of social and intellectual status. Having earned the highest educational and occupational level he has to continue to struggle to settle down. He learned Sociology and taught Sociology for nearly four decades. The story is one of three generations of his family, he being the first generation learner. The life story begins in the 1950s and ends with his retirement in 2015. The story is based on the insider's perspective from below with the efforts to identify and analyse interconnectedness of the facts of his life. The journey begins from a remote village and reaches the international level with academic and policy level contributions. I am sure there are several others like him in Indian society and some have already recorded such experiences. Believe me, this is a life story of a sociologist and by a sociologist.

2
Synopsis

Politically, the idea of India as a nation is quite recent. It is considered to be a very old civilization with a great rich cultural and religious heritage. Hinduism as a philosophy and religion is inherently woven into the Indian social and cultural fabric. Indians are thoroughly socialized and conditioned to attribute everything to God and religion; this includes the human body, mind, thought and act, which are further classified into the dichotomies of good and bad, pure and impure, high and low, heaven and hell and birth and rebirth. These further branch out into several specific notions and taboos around purity and pollution. The Hindu thought believes in rebirth and human birth which is considered to be an event that is attained after several births as other, lower life forms. However, the present birth into human life is attributed to one's deeds or karmas in the past life and further into different categories of humans: if you are born a woman, there is a negative reason attributed to your birth and if you are born into the lowest social rank of a society, a different negative explanation is given. Similarly if you are poor, it is because of your misdeeds in your past life. So the principle of birth and rebirth is applied to every act of yours. And all this occurs because of the great will of god(s), approved by religion, controlled by a small section of the population that is supposed to be superior, pure and capable. As a result, with the course of time, this thought has led to clear hierarchical and graded social divisions based on caste and gender. There have been some efforts in history to dismantle all these structures; however, they managed to survive till date perhaps due to the ignorance and inculcation of extreme religious orthodoxy imposed on the common masses besides a total lack of formal education for most of the population. Caste as an institution has been the strongest and healthiest form of religion that divides Indian society into four *varnas* with assigned unchangeable duties. Among the many theories on caste, this is the most widely recognised and accepted. These *varnas* are based on social hierarchy and the purportedly 'pure' and 'impure' dichotomies with vertical graded divisions. Each *varna* has several castes and sub-castes with all social, occupational, ritual and cultural differences and clear hierarchy and prescribed restrictions. At the bottom are the *Shudras*. The category of *Atishudras* (Untouchables) are so far below on the scale of caste hierarchy that they are out of the *varna* system. India as a country and also as a nation continues to face all these odds even in the current modern times. There have been some formal and informal efforts to reform Indian society during modern times, although it continues to be known as traditional, religious, diverse and complex. It is to be noted that a sizeable section of Indian society has been at the bottom, always born to serve, gets exploited and leads a pathetic life and was earlier termed 'untouchables' and is now referred to as *Dalits*, or the Scheduled Castes in official terms. The members of this caste remain neglected in many ways and continue to suffer discrimination and indignities of all kinds. Those who manage to emerge from this hell are few but continue to face new forms of discrimination and deprivation. It is pertinent to know their life history, their sufferings and struggle and success in an environment where human beings are still unimportant and God, religion, caste and gender triumph in all aspects of humanity.

This work is based on the life of a man who was born and raised in the community of Mahar (a caste of the untouchables). As an outcast, he led his life in pathetic conditions and yet achieved the highest educational degree and occupational status. Yet he still continues to struggle to come out of the social stigma of caste and untouchabilty even though he has managed to overcome poverty and join the middle economic class. When he looks back in life, he feels the past has been so unkind and so strong that it gets reflected in the present in many ways. This raises several questions that are addressed in this work: Has this happened in isolation? Have all his real life experiences affected his mind, emotional world, abilities and creativity? How and why do his dignity and self-respect suffer from a crisis? What does the future hold for him and his community? What happens to his family? Another issue that surfaces is that all his achievements appear to benefit only the individual and do not directly impact others who suffer in a similar way. The work simultaneously traces the exceptional and unexpected trajectory of his life. This journey is certainly attributed to modern forces including education, the reservation policy and to Dr. B.R. Ambedkar and his movement in particular. Moreover it also seeks to contemplate a scenario where Dr. Ambedkar had not existed. He is still considered a misfit member of the elite and the common people still perceive him as low and undeserving. The book seeks to examine the reasons for such a perception and the people who have propagated such a thought. The book is based on the real experiences and observations of this author's life, right from his childhood to the present stage of his life; from the village to cities to countries, tracing across generations the changes, and paradoxically, the continuities in social and economic situations in this country. Education, although highly inaccessible and unaffordable played a key source of motivation and change in transforming his life and improving his status propelling him into the modern, secular and respectable profession of academia. From the 1st standard till the 10th he used to work as a daily wager on holidays on the agricultural farms with half the wages paid to women to support his family. Walking 4 miles barefooted to the nearby village to attend school from the 5th to 7th standard. After school at home, every day in the evening before his mother comes home from work, he used to fetch water from the well, clean the house, wash utensils and go around the village to collect firewood for cooking. One such day, his left foot got badly injured while cutting a thick and long dry branch of a tree with the help of an iron grass cutting device. It was bleeding profusely with severe burning pains. He went back home. His mother prepared a turmeric solution, applied it on the wound covered with a piece of old cloth. Yelling and crying out from pain, he spent the night sleeplessly. Next morning the foot was swelling with more pain. He was unable to walk properly. At night he suffered from high fever. His mother covered his body with her old saris, patting his head and body with tears in her eyes. This continued for three days. It was a wonder he did not get infected by tetanus or any other major causality. The wound mark is still clearly visible on the foot. The dynamics of caste have had an impact even among the neo-liberals who abound in academia. There have been only a few individuals from the upper castes who indirectly and directly extended support and sympathy during his education and career. He took on the task of writing and recording his life experiences after his retirement as a professor of sociology at the age of sixty-five; however, the urge to write such a record has always been there from his youth. The prime intention of the piece of work is not to glorify, seek sympathy or directly blame or condemn anyone but make known to all those who believe and practise human values and fight for justice, equality and fraternity with a humble submission acknowledging the struggles of a fellow fighter. This is also written for those who do not believe in the values of humanity and equality. It is a matter of serious concern and a tragedy that still a majority of human beings in the world and in India, in particular continue to suffer from social, religious, ethnic and economic slavery.

3

Prologue: Why Do I Write?

Not everyone is fortunate enough to have lived the life I have led. Today, as a retired professor from a prestigious educational institution in India, I still continue to contribute to the world of academia and to the world of sociology. In my classes I have always told my students to voice their stories. The more deprivation they had overcome, the more important it was to find their voice and tell their own story so that it would help the ones treading similar paths to find courage, to find hope. Today, I think, perhaps my voice, my story, needs to be heard as well.

It is a story in many ways of triumph of will over circumstances, of the highs of friendships and humanity, of the lows of pettiness that one finds in the world, of the strength (and at times the misery) that can be, of the progress of India and of the need to go further.

The life story approach in sociology is an ethnographic one and traces the events and processes in one's life that shape one's development. The symbolism and regulations that society lives by that complement or contrast the meaning they have in an individual's life is now data for the sociologist. My interest is in trying to showcase this twining of the individual's story—my story, with that of society.

4

Where Do I Come From?

My Roots

Man is a social creature. The relationship between the individual and society is a complex one. This relationship, in fact, forms the basis of sociological enquiry. An individual shapes the society he or she belongs to. However, the norms of the society one is exposed to, influence the individual as well. One is often forced to conform to the rules and beliefs of one's society. Often, this conformity is an unconscious act. This is what we call conditioning. It is for this reason that, for a sociologist especially, no story can be exempt from the roots of an individual, the conditions surrounding an individual's actions or thoughts.

The Beginning

My life began with a zero. I was born into a poor untouchable (Mahar) family in a remote small village called Karla that is the last village in the west direction of Amravati district of Maharashtra state. Both my parents had no education at all and lived as landless labourers. My mother gave birth to 10 children: 5 sons and 5 daughters, with a 3 year gap between each. Among the 5 daughters, 2 were twins. Three of us sons surprisingly survived. The others, unfortunately, all died at infancy or during childhood; possibly due to some disease or more likely, malnutrition. I am the middle among the 3 with a 7-year gap of age between us. Serially, I am the sixth child.

I do not know my actual date of birth. This has, at times, led to problems during my studies or even at work. Those days were the early days of independent India. Children were born often than not born at home. Time was measured more by seasons and festivals and the day and time of birth was not meticulously recorded. Birth certificates were unheard of. Even in a village with just about a 100 households and around 500-700 population, records of births and death were not accurately maintained. Records, kept by the Patil (head) of my village, state that I was born on March 1, 1950. However, this merely means that I was likely born in late 1949 or early 1950 when someone bothered to register my birth as part of village data. The practice of assigning the first day of the month in a year to a child born is the norm across much of India till the 1990s when birth certificates became mandatory. My story began in the 1950s.

Colours of Caste

My village was not a large one. It used to be connected by a *kuchha* (mud) road to small towns in the east and west, one of them being Taluka Akot falling in Akola district. The two towns were the markets for major shopping to be done for major festive occasions, marriages, deaths, etc. The village had only a primary school. We needed to go outside the village to study beyond the 4th standard.

Even with just 100 households, there was a rigid clustering of houses based on the castes the people belonged to. Certain locations were for the 'upper caste' and some sections were cordoned off for the so-called lower castes. The village had one Brahmin family. The couple had 9 sons. This family used to perform all the rituals for all the castes other than the Scheduled Castes (SCs).

Most of the villagers belonged to the 'middle castes' such as the Malis, Kunbis and Marathas. There were also

3 or 4 barber families who never gave a haircut to the SCs. Then there was a carpenter household and one belonging to a blacksmith and a grocer household.

The occupations signify a caste hierarchy as well. Even within each primary castes (Brahmins, Kshatriyas, Vaishyas and Shudras) there was a sub-hierarchy that fostered a sense of privilege for those 'higher born'. The washerman's family would not service the untouchables and this custom continues even today. The tailor, carpenter and goldsmith would provide services to our community but would always maintain sufficient physical distance to avoid touching us.

The Maratha families were located at quite a height from the main grounds of the village. They owned huge tracts of agricultural land. Only they could be the head of our village. The families had a system of rotating the position so that each Maratha family had an equitable shot at being the head. The role of the head was to maintain law and order, resolve disputes and maintain records of village land, revenue, etc. Our village was known to be prosperous due to rich agricultural production. But the land was owned mainly by the Malis and Marathas. There was a popular saying for each caste expressing a deep meaning with qualities attributed to their status and prestige in the society; like—

Bamna ghari livnā, patla ghari lenā
kunbya ghari danā, mahara ghari ganā,

meaning—education goes with Brahmins, high living standard goes with Patils (Marathas), all agricultural product (prosperity) goes with Kunbis and song (singing) goes with Mahars.

Exactly on the eastern section of the village was the Maharwada. Its location ensured a significant gap between the 'upper caste' and 'untouchable' houses. The prevalent belief at the time was to house the Mahars on the eastern outskirts of the village. This was done so that the 'upper castes' would not be polluted by the winds carrying the scent of the Mahars, since the winds in western India blow from west to east. Relatively, it was the Maharwada that had the most number of households at that time, perhaps around 20-25.

Towards the north, but outside the village boundary was a household of a Mang family. And still further away, just outside the village lived a Chambhar family. There were 3-4 houses of the Kolhati community who specialized in prostitution that was socially sanctioned in the name of tradition.

During the 1950s-60s, a few families immigrated from other places and settled in a western corner at the entry of the village. They were known as Takonkar, repairing and making traditional grinding stones being their traditional occupation. They claimed to be socially superior to all the lower and middle castes, because they were originally Rajputs (as claimed by them), descended from Maharana Pratap who belonged to the royal family of Mewar. Their families had perhaps scattered across India after Maharana Pratap's defeat in the Battle of Haldighati in 1576.

The one room school was located on top of the *garhi* and had two teachers who were husband and wife belonging to the Brahmin caste. The village temple was known to be the Maruti (also known as Hanuman) temple located in the western direction of the village and had a Brahmin *pujari* who was a bachelor. There was no entry into the temple for Mahars, Mangs and Chambhars. Even God was rationed for those from the 'lower' fringes of society.

Epidemics were a frequent feature in the village. Cholera, smallpox, typhoid, scabies etc. used to be common. There were two temples outside the village in two different directions known as *Mari Maay* (Maay means mother) and

Mesu Maay. Mari Maay was the Goddess of Cholera and the Mesu Maay that of smallpox. The villagers used to believe that whenever these goddesses were annoyed with them the epidemic occurred. During the epidemic all villagers used to gather in a group and make music (traditional musical instrument made of leather by the Mang himself and beat it on the way till the temple). After reaching the temple the villagers used to collectively perform puja of the goddesses with all the drum music, puja offering her plate full of coconuts, new green coloured *choli* (blouse), green bangles and a few specially cooked sweets to please the goddess so that the epidemic would stop and people would not die. The goddess of cholera had a high roofed temple with the main idol and small idols at her left and right on the higher level from the ground. The idols were simply and roughly made of stone with *sindur* (vermilion) and oil thickly pasted on the idols. However, the untouchables were not allowed to enter the main temple and had a small open place with other idols placed outside the temple for worship. Songs would be sung by women folk to praise and please the goddesses. They used to sing songs at home and during processions and puja. Slowly the government health department located 10 miles away started deputing a doctor with 1-2 nurses known as *daais*. They used to treat the patients. All the patients would be brought to the school at the height of an epidemic. There used to be no classes during this time.

As children, we would find the used medical equipment around when school reopened, things like syringes, used soaps, dressing material, etc. Once I picked up a used soap out of curiosity as soap was a special and expensive item for our household. I wanted to take it home. But a classmate told me to throw it away and I did. I was perhaps in the 1st or 2nd standard at that time. Another social practice was using black magic by a particular man or woman to punish someone and/or an infertile woman to have a child. Getting possessed by a local god or goddess or male or female evil spirit was common.

The Maharwada: The locality of Mahars was known as *Maharwada* and was most like a ghetto. The Mahar caste was known for loyalty and bravery reputed to be special qualities of the caste. During the British period in India, the government established the Mahar regiment owing to the concerted efforts of Dr. B.R. Ambedkar that exists even today in the Indian Army. However, in society, the Mahars were shunned as the 'lower caste'. Their households were situated in the eastern outskirts of the village; small mud houses with local tiles in congested narrow lanes. A common well met the water needs of our community. Even if one wanted to change the system, one would have to take on the vicious all powerful panchayat (the village leadership). The panchayat's decisions were final and they could dictate terms on any issue from the socio-economic to the personal.

There were no toilets; rather men and women used the open space around the village but prominently closer to Maharwada since the wind direction was west to east and open defecation in the east would mean the 'upper caste' in their cosy, west-located homes did not have to suffer the stench. The Mahars, however, had no such respite.

Each household used to worship a particular family deity. Whether the deity was a god or a goddess, the deity would receive an animal (generally chicken) sacrifice. My family worshipped a male god (known to be the family deity) known as *bahiram* whose original open temple is situated on the top hill of Satpura hills range some 70-80 kilometres away from the village towards the east on the border of Madhya Pradesh. There used to be an annual *yatra* (fair) for this god for 5 continuous weeks. The people flocking to the *yatra* would hail from all communities, except Brahmins, but mainly consisted of the local tribals and the lower caste people. It is believed that the god actually was the god of tribes who would bless and fulfil people's wishes. The idol has been mainly made of *sindhur* (vermilion*)* with sweet oil as people are supposed to use as the main part of *puja* with flowers, scent sticks, dry coconut and some sweets. Since people would add to the shape of the idol with *sindhur* as prayed to the deity, the idol would grow huge in all directions. The grounds around the yatra were stained red with the blood of animals (goats and chickens) used to offer an animal sacrifice to please the god. The animal sacrifice practice was later, mercifully, banned. At the same time this was also the period for major sales and purchases of agricultural devices, bullocks and *puja* materials like dry coconuts, flowers and sweets. There were also several sources of entertainment set up around the grounds like touring cinemas with tents, tamashas, circuses, etc. Even people from the neighbouring state Madhya Pradesh used to attend the *yatra*.

Part of the customs surrounding the *yatra* was that a male Mahar would get possessed by the deity. Some people who were possessed used to expect and ask for special favours relating to marriage, property, birth, etc. Menstruating women were not to be touched—another practice of gender bias.

I was possessed while I was studying in the 8th standard and continued till I joined college. It was perceived to be auspicious in a way and not good for an individual's life as it has several purity pollution perceptions and practices besides fear of evil practices by others. While this was revered earlier, in the Ambedkar era in which I was brought up this was criticized as succumbing to superstition. Many in the community criticized my family for and me claiming that I was possessed. They argued that this was against Ambedkar's teachings. My father and elder brother did not appreciate me being possessed at all.

It is difficult for me to understand and analyse the matter even now. I used to be overcome with feelings of strange excitement, strange body movement and unclear murmuring besides losing control over my body and mind. I used to feel strange and filled with tension on all full moon and no-moon days. Perhaps I was highly sensitive to the atmosphere. Gradually, I came out of it. Despite everything, my family members, used to offer *puja* at the main centre of the deity; especially a newly married couple or when a new baby was born. A symbolic haircutting ceremony of the new born baby in the family was routinely organized till around 1960. Society, sometimes, seems to be built on the foundation of segregation. The Maharwada households were further socially divided into two clusters: the original inhabitants of the locality and those who had immigrated to the region, even if that had been centuries earlier. While it remains a mystery to this date about the origins of these 'newcomers', they were perceived as inferior with low morals as compared to the originals who were superior with high morals and were *khandani* deserving respect. So there was always inherent rivalry between the two groups. Our family faced social boycott by this so-called lower group several times. This actually was because of jealousy due to the job my father used to do called *kamdar*i. Kamdari was a government job at the lowest level with a very low salary. The actual duties were to attend to visiting government officials, reporting any death, crime, murder, theft, etc. to the police and conveying their messages to the villagers.

Kamdari was originally a part of *balutedari*. Dr.

Ambedkar had given a clarion call to abandon traditional caste-based menial jobs that offended human dignity. Everyone in the community came together to heed the call and abandoned *balutedari*. This is why they felt my father was betraying the cause by continuing with a job that was associated with *balutedari*. However by this time the nature of duties assigned to *kamdar* were secular and all clean, demeaning tasks had been eliminated from the job description. However, the community held my father's occupation against our family. Nobody used to talk to us for months at a time. We were barred even from fetching the drinking water from the well in the *mohalla* (locality). However, my father, though uneducated, was smart, intelligent and therefore was able to face all the ostracism successfully. The job of *kamdari* used to bring income to support the family, since we had little to no land and was also a means to defend self and family because of contacts in the police and revenue departments.

Balutedari and the Mahars: In colonial India, our entire village practised *balutedari* (roughly the Jajmani System) that apportioned each household's income from agricultural yields and other odd sources. Each caste had its functions prescribed by traditions and customs with strict observance of hierarchy, social distance and purity-pollution norms. Known as *balutedari bara baluta* (12 balutas); meaning 12 castes would be involved in offering services to the upper castes like the Marathas and Kunbis. Their caste-based occupations were: 1. Nhavi-Barber 2, Dhobi-Washerman 3. Kumbhar-Potter 4. Shimpi-Tailor 5. Sutar-Carpenter 6. Lohar-Blacksmith 7. Sonar-Goldsmith 8.Teli-Oil Presser 9. Brahmin-puja and other rituals and the untouchables like 10. Mahar 11. Mang and 12. Chambhar.

Balutehari is the base of the Indian village system that used to assure people's rights and duties in the village with a prescribed share in the agricultural products and small piece of land. This share was known as *vatan*. Mahar *Vatan* used to be allotted on rotation among the Mahar families and it was mandatory to practise this across generations. The Mahars and other untouchable castes were engaged in unhygienic occupations and had to serve the upper castes and maintain overall cleanliness of the village. The main jobs of the Mahars were to clean the streets (done mainly by women), to carry and convey messages to other villages like deaths, marriages, to the police patil/police in case of any criminal incidents, to assist the kulkarni (revenue clerk) to measure lands and resolve disputes. The opinion of the Mahar in any land disputes was considered to be the final one. They were to also guard the village at night, to dispose of the dead animals, to make *torans* (decorative door hangings) of mango leaves during marriage ceremonies of upper castes (again done mainly by women), attend to the Patil/revenue clerk/ officer/police any time during day or night on their visits, etc. These tasks were compensated by their traditional claims on agricultural food products based on the fixed caste-based share. The women and children used to go around to upper caste households begging for their rightful share of cooked food prepared the previous night and on the occasions of festivals and marriages. The upper castes had the right to deny the 'lower castes' food in case they were dissatisfied with the services rendered. During marriages and the annual *yatra* the men and women with children used to wait outside for food for hours together and only get whatever was left at the end. Children and women used to collect food from discarded leftovers in a nearby waste-food garbage spot. They used to fight among themselves over this food. I used to go with my mother frequently for such food hunts. I saw and experienced the shouts, abuses and humiliations by the upper caste people who were more involved in the ceremony and worried about being 'polluted' by the 'lower castes'. Sometimes they would serve us the food after everyone had eaten, but away from the main area of the function and taking extra care to avoid touching us. Often we had to carry our own utensils to eat or carry the food home. This discrimination of excluding the 'lower castes' from consuming the food at religious functions did not extend to the ceremony itself that required firewood. All 'lower caste' men and women collected firewood from the jungle. They would cut the thick dry wood into smaller pieces in huge quantities. This was very hard and painful work with no recognition.

Women and men also worked as landless labourers for wages on the agricultural lands of upper castes. Both men and women generally wore used clothes gifted by the upper castes. Their clothes used to be shabby with a distinctive bad odour and look making it easy to identify their caste. Women used to wear particular types of ornaments made of silver, but only those who could afford such jewellery. Their language used to be with an accent and a specific vocabulary that was typical of their caste. They were generally aggressive and abusive among themselves. Quarrels and physical fights were a common feature of everyday life. Quarrels among Mahar women were a spectacle peppered with vulgar and unmentionable words. The reasons for such fights could be very petty or genuine.

The village had two graveyards, one for the upper castes in the western direction and the other for the untouchables in the south of the village. All the castes practised of burying the dead. There was a huge *garhi* (fortress) with four huge pillars in four directions made of white solid mud situated in the centre of the village. Its function was presumed to be to guard the village. No one knew as to who built it or even when. There used to be a one room school on the plane ground of the *garhi* on top. Today we see nothing there as people started digging the *garhi* walls for mud to be used for building house walls and to repair mud houses owing to the to good quality of mud. It is totally plane now.

Dead Animals: It is beyond our understanding why these communities (including Mangs and not Chambhars) ate the flesh of dead animals. Mangs waited a distance to collect remains of the flesh parts, being socially lower to Mahars, and Chambhars. Chambhars used to take away or buy the skins of the animals from the Mahars keeping away from the Mahars and Mangs. There are four major castes among the untouchables in Maharashtra such as Mahars, Mangs, Chambhars and Dhors. Chambhars being on top followed by Dhors, Mahars and Mangs in descending order. Chambhars and Dhors practised untouchability with Mahars and Mangs; and Mahars with Mangs. There was no inter-dining. The Dhors were inferior to the Chambhars. Their occupation was to clean and dry the animal skins and sell them to the Chambhars to make footwear and other leather goods required for cultivating land. No one knows the history and its origin. Even if some of them were relatively better off owning a piece of land, they all took pride in sharing the flesh of the dead animals which used to be a strong prestige point during marriage proposals. The upper caste man informed to the Mahars about the dead animals in the village and the family in rotation of the duty would carry it out of the village keeping a long distance between the village and the spot where they would cut the animals. First of all, the family with first claim over would take out the skin with great difficulties but very carefully so that the skin could be sold to the Chambhar who would either sell the skins in the town or would himself earn it and make footwear. After this the skilled person only would put the *suri* (a big sized knife like device) into the body and carefully cut and remove the parts from inside body considered to be very special and more testy like the liver and kidney. Another important and delicious part of the body used to be the brain and tongue. To take the brain out of the hard head and skull used to be require great skill. Other parts of the body were then distributed according to the fixed share. They used to carry them home in large utensils or gunny bags. There used to be stray dogs, crows and vultures fighting around the spot where the animal was disposed. With leaking blood around the body, they used to carry home and further cut pieces to boil and cook. Some used to make a curry or roast it and the remaining pieces were cut and kept on a thick rope in front of the house to dry. Drying pieces (called *chani(s)*: cutting pieces of flesh into vertical six to ten inches with thinness (so to dry fast) would take a few days to stop emitting a bad smell and attracting flies and crows on or around it. The dry *chanis* used to be stored in big earthen pots for future and during rainy days it used to be helpful to eat it as a meal in the absence of food due to lack of wages. The *chains* after roasting or frying in a pan used to taste so good. Non-vegetarian (beef) was considered to be a special menu. We used to have it almost every weekly *bazaar* day and when there were guests. Mother used to roast pieces of beef as a very special item. We used to enjoy the delicious food. Only the Muslims who belonged to the *kasai* caste used to sell the beef coming from the nearby town.

I, of course, played a part in all the scenes with my parents and elder brother. A few years ago and even today, some people from the community in some parts of Maharashtra still eat the flesh of dead animals. This is based on my direct observation during my research field work. I remember, I was at my grandfather's home in the town. I may have been around five. One day a small cow cub died. My grandfather was informed to take it away and took me along. He dragged it to the spot, skinned it and cut the flesh into pieces, wrapped in thick cloth and put it on my head and asked me to take it home. I took it home. The blood dripped around my head and body. People on the way ran away from me. I used to feel bad and ashamed but could not help. Mother had delivered a baby just two-three days before and had no food to eat. Grandmother made pieces and roasted them and gave my mother the food to eat. She ate them and the next day the baby died. I also ate the roasted pieces with salt as there was no *bhakri* (local thick bread made of jawar which was the main food) available.

How can we analyse this as a social fact that no sociology or anthropology or psychology or economics can help explain in and of themselves. How to justify this flouting of anything that is humanity—this under destruction of human dignity? What could be the origin of this? How did they get into this and who must have forced them to do this (can one believe that it was out of choice?) is an issue that poses challenges to those who claim to be proud of India's long history of rich culture and traditions.

The Maharwada has a big common well as the only source for drinking water since time unknown. The well was renovated with concrete cement from inside and outside in 1959 by the gram panchayat with cemented floor around and water layout. This was done as a special programme activity under the SC improvement scheme. It has four wooden wheels to fetch water using long ropes. Children used to bathe there in the open and others washed clothes. However, since the last many years the well has gone totally dry as the water level has gone down so deep. Now water supply is through taps with limited quantity and a given time.

I am told by my parents that our family along with others travelled by bullock carts for two days to visit and there was no other source of transport, to perform *puja* and make purchases every year. The animal sacrifice was banned only after the famous saint Gadge Baba intervened and appealed to people and the government not to sacrifice animals. He being strong, an active social reformer and anti-superstitious, people and the government both followed his advice and the government imposed the ban. He also vehemently propagated cleanliness. Gadge Baba was from the lower caste (Dhobi) and a contemporary of Dr. Ambedkar. He also actively supported the movement led by Dr. Ambedkar for social movement for removal of superstitions and propagating cleanliness. Gadge Baba is highly regarded and is known for his contributions in many ways to the society. While studying in the 8th standard in a town, I used to get possessed by the *Bahiram Baba* (our male family deity) with a positive motto for the welfare of the family and people around. However, none of my family members liked and wanted it as it is considered not to be good for normal life and my elder brother was against it—an impact of the Ambedkar movement. Still then with several *pujas* and appeals to God, I came out of this phase after two-three years. Frankly speaking, I have no explanation for this nor was it something I used to do or show artificially or consciously.

Life was not all dreary. Even in times of poverty and deprivation, arts are an uplifter. The Mahars were known for the art of singing and performing *gammat* (performing folk art). A group of four-five artists: a singer, a dholkiwala (two-head hand-drum player), a protagonist, a comedian and/or a supporting actor. The protagonist would be a male impersonating a female singer-dancer. This was because women were traditionally not allowed to participate in theatre. This group of artists would go around several villages to perform against reasonable fees and used to enjoy prestige and status. They would sing songs mostly based on the Ramayana and Mahabharata, mainly written by the man known as *shahir* and some songs on their life conditions.

Gammat is a heritage art form that was also a kind of inherited occupation and was much appreciated by all the people in and around the region. Even the 'upper castes' had such groups of actors. The folk art though relevant and entertaining was linked to caste(s). However, the *gammat* performed by the Mahars was appreciated and attended by the upper castes as well.

Another major and regular source of entertainment for villagers used to be *gandhar* (dandar). This was restricted to only the 'upper caste' actors and was therefore limited to being performed in 'upper caste' locations. It was a mega celebration spanning five to seven days from Dussehra, the first festival in the rotation of Hindu festivals. Both men and women from all castes used to come and watch it till late at night sitting in the open space on the floor. Men and women from the untouchable community sat in a corner keeping an appropriate distance from the spot and other high caste people. The performance of the artists took place in a pandal of about nine-ten feet tall supported by bamboos. The ceiling cover was decorative and it had a thick net all around up to three-four feet tall. The background artists sat with their musical instruments on a dais made out of strong wood with ample length and breadth. In a row in front facing the audience a group of six artists stood horizontally in a row with alternate male-female position (actually all males) with makeup and colourful outfits.

They used to dance together moving back and forth with songs, bits of music and wooden sticks in one hand and in the other a colourful piece of cloth banging the sticks with each other and waving the cloth piece to left and right. All the songs were sung by the performers as devotees of Lord Krishna or Rama. They would also tell jokes and a few of the others played joker, hunter, drunkard, etc. Everybody enjoyed the discourse with real enthusiasm.

Yet another specialty of the *gammat* group of artists was to organize and perform a play on the Ramayana. They themselves did everything from script to dialogues to songs, writing to singing and music. All female roles were performed by males. My father was one of the artists and performed any role required. This used to attract a huge crowd in the village and was also received in the villages around with great appreciation.

However, we find a sudden change in the themes and contents of all the songs and plays : from the Ramayana to the life of Budhha or Ambedkar, after the mass conversion move by Dr. Ambedkar in 1956. Those singing songs on the themes of Hindu religion would be criticized sharply; sometimes this criticism led to the social boycott of the artists. Art and politics are not divorced from each other. They may be independent of each other, but they are definitely influenced by the other. Perhaps my father's talent for art and his performances somewhere sowed the seeds for my passion for arts. Just as the *gammat* was influenced by societal mores and had to adapt to society's changes, so too I found societal expectations a yardstick by which I had to live. The arts are not free.

Blood Ties

Childhood: I am the middle son in my family and have 2 living siblings. My mother gave birth to 4 children after I was born, although two sisters born after me died during childhood. I remember clearly that my mother delivered each baby in the same tiny dwelling with the help of the traditional *dai* and other women in the village. The two sisters born after me died during childhood—the younger one was just six months old and the elder one four or five years. The elder one died of jaundice for sure because I vividly recall my father giving her the traditional medicine mixed in buttermilk. One fine morning, my mother and I left her alone at home to go and buy buttermilk and returned to find her dead. My brother, Sahdev is seven years older than me and was, along with some other friends from the community, the very first to answer the call for education given by Babasaheb Ambedkar. The tenth sibling, the youngest, is Prakash, who leads a happy life has retired recently from the PWD department. As is the eldest one. Both are married and have grandchildren. The elder got his MA and LLB degrees but the younger one could not clear his class 10 examination despite availing of all the given attempts. The most prominent reason for his failure was that children were promoted to upper standards even when they had actually failed. English as a subject was introduced only from the 8th class. And more importantly, he has been thoroughly pampered by my parents.

It is pertinent to write about my childhood experiences in the family as it shaped my motivations and actions. Being the middle child, I was neglected by my father, mother and elder brother. My parents lavished more attention, love, and care to the elder and the younger ones. Often my mother used to give my elder brother special food with or without my knowledge. Physical beatings were a regular feature, administered by my father and elder brother in particular. He was dominating and a much loved son of my parents. He was never questioned by any one. Despite being a student of Sociology, I have not been able to fathom his harsh, unkind behaviour towards me. When my elder brother scolded and beat me no one would stop him. My left ear still pains and is weaker compared to my right one that is entirely due to the hard slaps he gave me. I would feel so isolated and neglected that I remember thinking perhaps I was not their real son. I would often have the urge to run away or end my life.. One incident particularly stands out in my mind. I was beaten severely over a quarrel between my younger brother and myself. It was at night with darkness all around and there were strong wild stray dogs around. That day I ran away out of fear and hid behind a heap of agricultural yields in a neighbour's field where I fell asleep crying. When I woke up, it was midnight. I was very scared. My family members had apparently been looking for me all over the village. They thought I had jumped into a well to die. Finally they got tired and felt helpless and decided to wait till the morning. In the meantime, I do not know why, I started walking towards home without thinking. Reaching home, I was received by my *aatya* (aunt); she held me close, gave me a glass of water and asked me where I had gone. I told her everything between sobs. I was very attached to *aatya*. She was the only one who cared for me and loved me. These might be the feelings of an overwrought child and perhaps my parents cared for me in their own way. I could have been wrong in gauging their feelings. If so, I ask for their pardon.

Father had inherited two acres of agricultural dry land that used to give very little yield due to the bad quality of soil. Almost half the land was covered by big mango trees. There was not enough money to cultivate. Actually, this was just a piece of land from my grandfather's originally large property.

Inherited land was traditionally, at each generation, divided among the families. The sizable original share of land with good quality black soil was grabbed by a distant cousin for Rs. 100 (silver coins in British currency) from grandfather with an oral agreement for lending the money against mitigation of land for marrying the younger sister. After the marriage took place he could not return the money on time and the land was lost. The clan was supposed to have descended from a man called Sambhaji, though nothing much was known about him. My grandfather had one brother and 3 cousins. All of them were the present generation at the fourth-fifth level. He had one son (my father, Gangaram, was born in 1910, as per his version) and two daughters. His immediate brother had one son who had a daughter from his first wife who divorced for an unusual reason: she tried to talk and select the bangles directly with a wrapped sari after her bath. As mentioned by my father, my grandfather was literate and used to read *Pothi* and fast every Saturday. He tried hard to send father to school but he refused to go. Being the only son, he was pampered and never encouraged to do better. After my grandmother died in the cholera epidemic, they were brought up solely by my grandfather.

The kaka (my father's first cousin), married for the second time. He had a substantial amount of land and was relatively better off financially with many assets. But this couple, despite several efforts involving both traditional rituals and modern medicines, remained issueless. After confirmation that Kaku had a problem in conceiving, they adopted a girl who was Kaka's granddaughter, that is from the married daughter of his first wife. This girl studied together with me up to the 7th standard. She died of some unknown disease even after expensive medical treatment. She and I had appeared for the 7th standard board exam and both of us passed. But she died before the results were declared. Kaku and Kaka used to keep their distance from all of us. They would discriminate and differentiate between their adopted girl and me and my brothers. They never lacked goods or money but never shared it with us. On festive occasions and feasts, they would eat food behind a closed door and avoid us at every step of daily life.

My mother's name was Anusaya. She was good looking, light-skinned and slim. She was not very strong physically. She was a daughter of the Telgote family from Akot taluka, Nandipeth which had historical importance during both Muslim and British rule. Akot has nine Ves (localities) with Maharwadas in each Ves. Nandipeth was known for its famous Nandi temple and had a predominantly Muslim community with substandard conditions. Telgote was the only Mahar family in Nandipeth. All the Maharwadas have a common surname-Telgote. Mother's parental family was relatively well-off financially. They owned a piece of land and enjoyed a good status. My mother had two brothers and two sisters. Her maternal origin was not known to me.

Mother was married at an early age, probably before puberty. Grandfather was alive. She had the first girl child when very young. Grandfather died at this time. He was religious and literate. He used to fast on Saturdays and read pothi of the *shani* god. However my father was rather abusive towards my mother. Beatings and offensive words were commonly meted out to her. In spite of this my mother was very cooperative and submissive. She would work hard and earn from daily wages besides doing domestic work, caring for children and working for *balutedari*.

When we were young, my father's elder sister, *aatya* came to reside at her *Maher* (parental house) with her husband and five daughters. This was because she had lost many children just after child birth at her husband's place.

They all lived in a small *osari* attached to our small mud house. She had no son, only 5 daughters and we were 3 brothers with no sister alive. So all of us grew up as real siblings.

I have been told, I was an attractive light-skinned child with good health and was a great favourite of my cousins. They would bathe and feed me and dress me like a girl. I would imitate their language, actions and behaviour and act feminine. To some extent I continued to behave effeminately even after I grew up.

My father's younger sister, *aatya,* was married and visited us occasionally. Her husband was in the British army as a soldier, hence relatively better off financially. One fine day he converted to Christianity. After his conversion, my *aatya* had to face many problems. She was not allowed to go to her husband's place as he got converted. This went on for a few years. Finally she was allowed to go. But she and her children all started practising Christianity. After some time elapsed, however the relationship resumed between the two families. Whenever she visited us, she would bring several things for us, like food, money, clothes, etc. I was her favourite and often she would ask my father to let me go with her. My father, however strongly opposed this. Otherwise I would have been a Christian and have an altogether different life, education, job and thereby a different identity and existence. Finally, *aatya* and her family were distanced and in a way boycotted by all of us. To convert to another religion was perceived as anti-social; it was against norms and was considered a stigma. In those days the Christian missionaries (may be the Protestants) would strive to convert the untouchables. They visited villages with the converted locals and a British priest. They travelled in a jeep with food packets, biscuits, clothes and medicines for these people and give them with an appeal for conversion. A few of them around the district got converted. People in our village strongly opposed the conversion.

My father often spoke of his mother and her family. She was a widow living alone with a vast property. She possessed gold, silver and real British silver coins bearing Queen Victoria's image in three-four containers besides owning a sizeable amount of agricultural land. She had employed a manager to look after the property who eventually murdered her. All the net property was then grabbed by the police and the British officer. She had only one daughter (my father's mother) and after her death the remaining property was to go to my father as heir. But the offer was refused by my grandfather on ethical grounds. Finally the property was distributed among several relatives. Both my paternal and maternal families were traditionally part of the *balutedari* with every right and share in the village set up that were assigned by the caste system. For example, a Mahar man used to be a village watchman and messenger to other villages and to the government departments over good and bad news and emergency happenings. He also had a share over annual crops after harvesting.

My mother did all the domestic work, cooked food and worked for wages regularly. Fire wood for cooking was the main problem for her because there was no time for her to go to the jungle/roadside to collect dry branches or cut thick wood from trees. Somehow she would manage. At times my father used to bring firewood for her. I too would help her get firewood. I often helped my mother (never father and elder brother) in domestic work like collecting cow dung for *sarvan* (smearing) the space in front of the house with the dung, bringing firewood, fetching water from the well, washing utensils and clothes, etc. I was laughed at and made fun of, for doing women's work. If my mother fell sick, no one in the home would help her except me. I often washed her *saris* when she fell ill. Being a male and washing a woman's *saris* used to be against the customs of the time. Indeed, it was taboo so I faced many snide comments and people would make fun of me. There was not a single female in the house who could help her, so I used to feel sympathetic and help her as and when I could. I was attached more to my mother than my father. In addition, I also worked and earned half the wages of an adult female worker. The wages would be compensation for agricultural work on land owned by the upper caste/landlord and would involve having to remove the wild grass or weeds from the crops (nindan), collecting cotton and such. The black soil of the land there is very fertile, depending mainly on rains and the major crops were jawar and cotton. During harvesting season, all of us had good days to eat, work and live because both work and food was plentiful. The most difficult days were the rainy seasons and hard summer—April to May. Then there would be no work and no money. At times we would all go hungry, Mother sometimes prepared a liquid made out of a small amount of jawar flour known as *lapsi* and we would drink it to fill our stomachs and go to bed. My mother, however, would sleep on an empty stomach and the next morning go out in search of work. Father would also manage without meals. He was a fair, healthy and good looking man. He used to eat any kind of food leftovers or dry pieces of *bhakri*, made of jawar. I never saw him fall sick till he died at the age of 84 in 1990. Jawar roti (bhakri) is the main food in this part of Maharashtra. Poor Mahars generally dried the food in the sun whenever it was cooked in excess at home or collected out of leftovers from the village. This was stored for the hard summer and rainy seasons. The small dry pieces of *bhakri* are called *korke* in local language. They were stored in a mud pot, to be used as an alternate for regular meals in the absence of proper food, especially after the traditional occupations were given up and the dead animal flesh was discontinued from eating.

From the inside our house was sparse and shabby. A small mud wall—3' by 3'—divided the kitchen and the rest of the house. The wall was used to keep a small kerosene lamp and to ensure privacy for the kitchen. There were two vertical rows of big earthen pots attached to the mud wall and close to the kitchen spot (*chool*) to store groceries and raw food; although most of the time they were empty. Next to this there were 2-3 damaged trunks kept on a four legged wooden stool mostly filled with old disposable items. There were some gunny bags and old thick sheets of clothes used as bedding hung on a horizontally hanging bamboo. The other wall was used for hanging clothes meant for daily use. Our other meagre possessions included an old steel bucket to fetch water from the well, a few aluminium plates to have meals, 2-3 aluminium glasses and one big brass plate for making *bhakri*. Most of the utensils used were made of clay (known as shikori) including a big bowl to bathe. Soaps for bathing and washing were considered a luxury.

Hard work was a part of everyone's daily life in our family. For most of his youth and into his old age, my father collected good quality of firewood from the jungles to sell at the bus stand to people sitting there in groups. Whenever needed he would also do menial labour like loading and carrying of heavy items: bundles of firewood, vegetables, food grains, etc. meant for sale in the town or loading and unloading luggage of passengers, at the bus stop. This needed great physical strength and I have seen him doing this a number of times. I would feel ashamed while going to the school in the nearby village. Financial crisis was a regular feature in our household and buying new clothes used to be a big problem for all of us, whenever we needed some extra money.

At this point I would like to explain the role the Samta Sainik Dal (SSD) played that was instrumental in changing the lives of people in the Mahar community and consequently my family as well.

Samta Sainik Dal: Those were the heydays of Dr. Babasaheb's social movement. The main task of the Samta Sainik Dal (SSD) was to keep a strong watch on the Mahars and their traditional occupations besides focusing on the education of children and not follow Hindu practices but only Buddhist practices advised by Dr. Ambedkar in the conversion ceremony at Nagpur in 1956. The SSD members visited villages to check that no one followed the traditional occupations as per the message by Babasaheb to give up demeaning work and educate the school-going children. The impact of this move was so deep and effective that all the Mahars gave up their occupations overnight and almost all the children were enrolled in the school. I was one of them. However there were repercussions too. All the Mahars were boycotted strictly for two months and they were not given daily wages and denied access to shops and flour mills. Everyone suffered immensely during those two months. A Muslim zamindar from a nearby village used to come with a truck and take along all the men and women for wages to his land. These people would then buy all the basic necessities from there only. The village was under tremendous tension and the situation was full of conflict and crisis. Finally, the famous Republican Party leader Mr. R.S. Gawai and his team intervened. He came to the village and met the important upper caste people there. Somehow he facilitated a meeting between upper caste leaders and Mahar representatives together with Gawai and his team in the Maharwada to show that caste, untouchability and discrimination no longer exist. After extensive discussions on topics such as freedom, democracy, Dr. Ambedkar's philosophy and the social evils like untouchabilty, all the upper caste leaders were served water and tea by the Mahars. This was a grand historical event not only in my village but all around the region. I do remember I was sitting in the audience and as a small child, this incident had a deep impact on my mind. This was something great, new and unbelievable—the upper class men drank water and had tea in the Maharwada served by the Mahars. This was a major turning point in the life of Mahars and other SCs in general.

Some of the other changes ushered in by this change in attitude were the introduction of proper medicines in the community. Before that health and diseases were solely considered the domain of angry gods and goddesses and no real treatment was given. Dysentery (especially during the rainy season), malaria, typhoid, small pox, scabies, etc. were the common diseases. Whenever any member in the family got infected with small pox, the goddess of the disease was worshipped with special songs sung to appease her. The patient was covered with *neem* leaves and small idols made of cow dung were placed in the house and worshipped. There was no modern medical treatment as there was no doctor in the village and neither was there any awareness of modern medicine. During the course of time, a Primary Health Centre (PHC) was established in a nearby village with a compounder who used to give some medicine for routine sicknesses. He was from Rajasthan, a Marwadi. Otherwise for every routine or serious illness, people used to self-medicate and in serious cases they were taken to the taluka place for treatment. There was absolute ignorance about health along with an inability to afford the cost of a doctor and the medicine.

Beef Eating: The SSD used to keep a firm watch and force people not to follow traditional occupations, not to eat dead animal flesh and send their children to schools and not to ask/beg for food leftovers. May be noted, among the Mahars, the *vatan* used to be on rotation among the families on an annual basis and had first right over the dead animals and over the leftovers of food. Those who dared not follow this would face social boycott or serious quarrels between the families.

The British rule then changed the revenue system and appointed new officials such as *patwari,* revenue officer, *tahsildar* and the *kotwal* to serve all the officers including reporting to them and be an important and authentic witness in the case of land disputes. However, after the SSD's intervention, to work as *kotwal* was treated as low and degraded as he was to perform all low level duties with no formal appointment. My father continued to work as *kotwal* even after the strong objection by the SSD because then it became a feature of a regular job with prescribed salary of Rs. 7 that time with modifications in duties. Generally my father did not take on hard and manual work. As a consequence, father and our entire family was boycotted several times and caste fellows used to criticize, condemn, and ridicule to the extent that all the others would even stop talking to us and stop all exchange including emergencies. Of course there was an element of jealousy and rivalry behind their coldness. Even Kaka and his wife would join the other group. I used to be ridiculed and humiliated by my friends over this. At times I used to feel isolated and never understood the logic behind their behaviour. After 6-7 years of service my father's salary was increased to Rs. 16. The salary was paid on a monthly basis at the *tahsil* office in the town. He had to travel by bus/ bullock cart to collect it. By the time it was considered a secular government job with no stigma but the Mahar villagers' social stigma.

Branching Out: The First Step to Success

The school in our village consisted of one room and was on top of the *garhi* with four classes up to the 4th standard. This primary section had two teachers. I do not remember exactly the day or the time and procedure of getting admitted to the school. I vaguely remember my father with other Mahars taking a group of five-six children with my Kaka's granddaughter to the school. No one, however, is sure of my date of birth. My date of birth seems wrongly recorded by a year or two that affected my services at the time of retirement. When quizzed, my mother would oscillate between summer and winter with equal uncertainty. The formally recorded date is March 1, 1950.

My elder brother was already going to school with his caste fellows along with upper caste boys. He was 4-5 years ahead of me. Most of the boys from other castes and the Mahar caste were enrolled in the school. Only a few girls from upper castes were enrolled with us. However, children from our caste going to school was something very new and special as a result of the movement led by Dr. Ambedkar and the practical follow up of the SSD.

All the students in rows with class-wise divisions used sit in one room but the Mahar students would sit in a group separately. Girls of course sat separately from boys. The lady Brahmin teacher used to bring water to drink in a big bowl. We never drank water from her bowl and if someone tried, the high caste children would stop them. The school had no urinal/toilet facilities. Everyone was required to run home whenever needed. During the break we would go home to eat. The lady teacher and her husband teacher were very strict and known for severe physical punishments. Many students avoided going to school or ran away or dropped out of school. No parents would object to their punishments; rather many of them encouraged and appreciated it. The lady teacher would handle the classes up to the second standard. The first standard curriculum was to learn and practise drawing lines on the slate in the vertical, horizontal and diagonal directions and count them orally in a loud voice together. She would draw the lines on the blackboard and we copied it on our slates. There was a book prescribed for standard one. It had some pictures and alphabets printed and lines to learn. Whenever the teachers complained to parents, we would get beaten at home. I remember passing every class on the borderline. After reaching the 3rd standard the guruji (teacher) taught *padhe* (tables), poetry, writing and maths. Everyone had to recite all the poems with actions. If anything went wrong the guruji used to cane us with a solid wooden stick, and pull our hair and ears and insult students in the class. One day when I was in Standard 4, I was beaten so badly that I could not sit or walk properly. The mistake was that I was slightly late to school. Besides that, wearing a Gandhi cap was compulsory and everyone had to have their hair cut very short. That day my hair was a bit longer, at home I got engaged in setting and combing my hair by looking into the water-filled earthen pot (meant for drinking water). In those days film actor Dev Anand was very popular. The hair was not getting set properly and I kept setting it and forgot the time and the cap to wear. After reaching school, the guruji called me and started beating me severely. He made fun of my imitating

Dev Anand. All the students started laughing at me. I was crying and shouting in pain but no one came to my rescue. I still remember the beatings and the pains I suffered then.

In the 4th standard, we had old basic maths with additions, subtractions, multiplication, poetry recital, grammar, essay writing, etc. Marathi poetry used to be written by classical old poets with dedications to God, romance of Nal-Damayanti or story of Shravan baal but with very high old classical Marathi difficult to read and comprehend. In the 4th standard we had to sit for a board examination. There were special efforts from the school to prepare students for the exam, as there was no concept of private tuitions. The learning objectives were to acquire language, reading and writing skills with fluency and clear and proper pronunciation, mathematical skills, memorization skills and basic understanding of geography and history. But the examination was known to be very tough to pass. It was conducted by a specially appointed Inspector by the school board committee who would come from the board office located at Nagpur.

The year would pass with *Diwali* and other routine holidays. I used to study and also work with my mother to earn wages on the agricultural farms on weekends after half-day's school and followed by the Sunday and weekly bazaar days. The memories of discrimination are clear: the ladies from other castes also worked as labourers on the farm but maintained a distance, avoiding physical contact of all the low-caste women and keeping food and water separate. Once unknowingly I touched the vessel of the woman worker from the upper caste. She was so furious, that she started abusing and cursing and finally she angrily broke the earthen pot into pieces and remained without water for the whole day. I felt humiliated and was unable to understand the meaning behind it. Later I came to know that the woman was actually a sophisticated prostitute living with an upper caste rich man.

The wages for work were received only on bazaar day once a week. Father used to collect the money from the employer or the middle level contractor directly that was a big relief for my father. Then going to the nearby village for the weekly bazaar to buy things for the entire week, that used to be generally grocery, *paans-nuts* (betel), chewing tobacco, some green vegetables, a few *daals* (lentils) and some sweets for the children. In addition, some dry fish (bombils) and a kilogram or one *sher of* beef. The bazaar day used to be special for all the people as there was festivity with sweets and non-vegetarian meals on that day. We could not afford goat mutton. Sometimes father used to buy goat mutton at a low price for parts like *vajadi, rakti or khur* (offal) because others would not buy such degraded parts of the meat.

Finally, the 4th standard board examination approached. We were all ready. The exam was to be held at the nearby village two miles away as the centre for the exam. We were to walk two miles to reach the centre early in the morning. All upper caste rich boys and girls were to travel by bullock cart and carry food to eat at noon. We the SC boys and my Kaka's daughter along with 2-3 more boys decided to start walking early in the morning. It was a hot summer day. Mother woke me up very early in the morning. I bathed with cold water and prayed. Mother gave me something to eat. Father gave me 4 *annas* to buy and eat something at noon. None of us carried food since we did not have any. Finally we started and reached the centre on time.

The exam centre was ready and the Inspector was very strict and highly religious with a *tilak* on his forehead. Before the exam started we had to say a prayer.There was a water drum kept outside the room to drink water with a glass meant for others and a separate big bowl for all SC students. The exam started right on time with the written question paper followed by an oral test, reading test, maths and poetry recitation. There was a break at noon for lunch. All the teachers and students assembled to have their lunch. The other caste fellows and I went to the nearby small tea *dhabas* to eat *bhajiyas* and tea. I was very curious and attracted to see and buy grapes that I saw for the first time in life. I bought them for one *anna*. It was filling enough to eat and be satisfied. Holding them in both hands, I was thrilled and started running to show them to my friends. It was a blazing hot noon, and the paths were thick with dust. As I ran, I slipped and fell. The grapes flew out of my hands and spread all over in the dust. My knees and feet were full of scratches and blood. I rose with difficulty, feeling bad about losing the grapes and embarrassed to make a spectacle of myself. I remained quiet. My friends had a great time laughing at me. At the end, I went hungry the whole day. After appearing for the exam at noon, I walked back home in the evening on an empty stomach. The exam continued for 3 days. So we finished the board exam. My cousin and I were very apprehensive about the results. However, after a month the results were declared. Both of us passed the exam. I passed on the border. The great thing to remember in life and the school system then was that in the 3rd standard, one lesson was on the topic as to why sea water is salty in a story form. The answer at the end was that the heroine of the Arabian Nights story was grinding salt at the bottom of the sea and hence the sea water is salty.

I have another memory from those school days: while in the 2nd standard, a lesson on the thirsty crow led me put in a few stones in the big well in the Maharwada with a full amount of water to see the water level go up the way the water level in the pot went up after the thirsty crow put in some stones. The results of my experiment were frustrating. I was wondering why the water level did not increase. There was no one to guide, explain or correct me. I mentioned this to my father and mother who had no answers. My brother was away in town to study.

During the school days, proper clothes used to be a major problem. It was not possible to afford new clothes or proper books. To always wear the same one half-pant and the shirt to be washed without soap and wear the same again was the routine. Even the new plain cloth bought for new clothes, was of poor quality. The stitching charges would be too much, even when my parents pooled their earnings. Once I insisted that my father buy me a new bush shirt and kept crying for it for hours together, hugging him. He was just silent without any reaction or comments. Finally I gave up and calmed down. My mother and father faced the same problem. At times, mother approached the upper caste rich women for *saris* and at times she would get them and use them. Alternately father used to buy her old used *saris* from the weekly bazaar. She would be happy with that. But women around her ridiculed and looked down on her. She would just ignore them. I remember father never used such old shirts or *dhotis*.

After passing the 4th board exam, everyone in the family was happy and enthusiastic for me to study further. But there was no school after the 4th in the village. It was at Bhandaraj, two miles away from my village and where a weekly bazaar was also held. There was a road made by the PWD department but it was half kucha and half pucca with tar. The school was a Zilla Parishad school from the 5th to 7th standard.

One fine day, I went with my father to the school with the required certificates and got enrolled in the 5th

standard. Here it was tougher than the village school known for good trained teachers with very strict discipline. Except one SC (Chambhar) teacher, all of them were Brahmins including the headmaster. Also, they were all males. The school started in June. I was ready to start going but had no school uniform and could not afford it either. The teachers punished me several times for this. I was often asked to stand outside the classroom or to go back home and punished physically. Somehow my father managed to get the uniform for me. In the new school, I learned the great English alphabets for the first time. Maths, history and geography were very tough subjects for me and I would score low marks and get punished.

The days were enthusiastic and also hard. Enthusiastic because all the village students, including juniors and the seniors from the SC community, the two-three upper caste girls and my cousin, used to walk the four miles a day to and fro. Some barefooted, like me, on the road that was full of hard and sharp stones laid down for construction of road. Part of it used to be covered with tar, while some had solid sandy mud. We used to start early and reach the school at 10 am. On the way, both sides of the road were full of wild green trees, bushes, mango trees, tamarind trees and a few wild fruit trees. We would collect and eat those fruits as per season. Some of the skilled children would climb the trees to collect fruits. I never did it, I was scared and unskilled. The roads were flanked by fields full of edible crops. . I remember that the boys would take extra care of girl students for security reasons.

Most of them chewed tobacco and *paan* and smoked *bidis* on the way. In the company of these students, I too picked up the habit of chewing tobacco and paan. At times there used to be fights among them for some or the other reasons. Carrying bags full of books and notebooks besides

Shidori (lunch with *bhakri* and *bhaaji* packed in a piece of cloth) for lunch at school used to be heavy work. Those days the private transport buses carrying passengers had been recently introduced. We always tried to travel by bus free of cost. Some bus conductors were accommodating and some, not. One Sindhi owner of a bus was known to be very strict and never allowed any student to board his bus. After some time, the public state transport buses started providing service between towns, but we still could not ride in those buses. One day a kind bus conductor allowed 3-4 of us to board the bus to our village. After reaching the village, the bus stopped to allow the passengers to alight. He got out of the bus to manage the passengers, leaving his ticket kit behind. While he was busy, we took out as many tickets as we could from the kit and hid them in our bags. This was more out of curiosity than with the intention of playing a prank. We never paused to consider that. The poor conductor must have been punished by his boss and must have paid the cost of the tickets from his pocket. We got out of the bus delighted with our stolen haul and playing with them till all the tickets were destroyed and thrown away.

Generally, I would not have any food to eat during the break. The others would sit in the small garden of the school and eat their lunch. Some students shared food with me, but mostly, we were shunned. Some of them were liberal enough to allow us to touch their food and water bowl. However, the school had a common drinking drum where there was no objection to sharing. But a few of them, especially girls, used to scream if we used it.

The students had to clean the open spaces and water the ground and garden. There was a complete absence of entertainment and extracurricular activities. No picnic, no annual day, no feast. Only teaching and learning and examinations. The headmaster insisted on Sanskrit prayers at the beginning and end of the school. In this school too, there were no toilet facilities. We relieved ourselves in the open or by the *nalah*. Girls went to the houses of local girl students to use wash rooms and toilets. Another Brahmin teacher was a popular teacher; he taught English and Maths. He had leprosy but no one bothered.

Here too, the teachers gave hard physical punishments of all kinds. The most severe punishments given were by a SC teacher who also abused us. A few of them lived in nearby villages and commuted every day to school. One student in my class was very smart looking. His mother was a prostitute who danced in *Tamasha*. The boy claimed to belong to the upper caste and never apologised for being the son of a prostitute.

This school had classes from 5 to 7. Thus, three years passed with success till the end of the year at the 7th: when the annual examination approached. This was again a board exam known to be very tough to pass. Again, with written and oral tests conducted by a Board Inspector. Somehow I managed to pass with minimum marks. My cousin also passed. Her marks were not known because no one bothered to know. She died of some unknown disease after the exam despite the doctor's treatment that was given only when she was dying. Till then she was under local treatment and depending on faith in gods and goddesses who were offered *navas* by her grandmother. It was really a tragic death. She and I studied together under a kerosene lamp from the first standard. No one guided us or enquired after our studies, we were on our own. Parents and neighbours liked and admired us for our study and hard work and expressed full trust in us. To go to school and be educated was a great feat for the people that time because everyone was uneducated.

Given those days of the 1960s and the existing social, economic and educational environment, getting up to the 7th standard was a miracle and worthy of admiration. However, the success story up to this level was limited to a very few boys/girls as the system of education and the social environment were highly unfavourable; especially because of the distance between the school and homes and the harsh treatment meted out at the school. Only 4-3 boys passed the 7th while the remaining failed and dropped out permanently. While in the 7th, a classmate, an upper caste girl was married while studying. From the SCs, we 3 survived up to the 7th standard. Two of them got up to graduation, another committed suicide due to a petty quarrel with his mother and the third, who is my second cousin turned blind owing to lack of vitamin A and now begs for a living. My brother and myself have been the only survivors till postgraduation level and beyond.

The real source of motivation behind our educational success and mobility have been my father and mother. Father seemed to have taken a pledge to educate us against all odds. The small piece of land he had inherited from his father, as well as the tiles and wooden pillars of our ancestral house were sold to meet our educational expenses. He wanted us to get educated up to the highest level and work in good government jobs so that others would look at him with respect and honour.

Joining High School: Father and brother both decided to send me to Akot to join high school. Akot is an old historical taluka town in the district of Akola. It is 10 miles away from my village Karla in the west. It had both public and private transport facilities with a pucca tar road. At that time it also had 3 high schools and a college, all private and aided by the government. There was bifurcation of the streams at the 9th standard: Arts and

Science. I joined Arts because science was more expensive and hard to study. There were two schools for boys and one for girls. The high school had the standards from 8th to 11th. In those days the students had a choice between doing the secondary level (10th) or could do one more year or 11th standard known as higher secondary. The latter was considered to be very tough. After passing the 11th, the student would directly join the first year degree college. Those joining the secondary, i.e. the $10^{th,}$ would need to do a one year pre-university course from senior college and then join the degree course. I joined the 10th and then joined the one-year pre-university course. The high school I joined was Shivajee High School where my elder brother had studied before me. It is located right on the road side of the Karla-Akot links. The school was a branch of the Shri Shivajee Education Society founded by Shri Punjabrao Deshmukh who belonged to the Maratha caste and was a popular Congress leader and social activist in the Vidarbha region. There were several schools and colleges run by the Society under his leadership in the region. The main objective of the Society was to spread education among the common masses as a social cause.

The school was only for boys. It had fully trained teachers and administrative staff. I do not think they had a reservation policy meant for SC-ST. However, there were many students from these communities studying from local and nearby villages. My cousin's husband actually enrolled my name for the 8th by paying the required fees and submitting documents. He was a local resident and was semi-educated. His occupation was to distribute newspapers. Akot was a place of my mother's parents. So my Mamas (maternal uncles) and other relatives were also from Akot. It was also a centre for shopping, had medical doctors, etc. The school had no hostel facility and the school uniform was compulsory.

My elder brother was studying at the college in the same town. While he was at college before I joined him, he also stayed in a private rented room. Father sent him meals through a Muslim driver who drove a private passenger bus. Sometimes the bus would be late or leave early and my brother would miss his meal. Father decided to hire a room so that both of us could stay together. It would also be economical. A room was found at the rent of Rs. 7 per month, in the Khanapur Ves. It was fully a Maharwada. Due to financial constraints and the distance between the school and my uncle's home, we decided to stay on rent and avoid any souring of relationship. My cousin also lived in the same locality. All of them had a hand-to-mouth existence. So to avoid being a burden and pressure we chose to live away from them. Aatya was called to cook for us. The room was fairly small with a *chulah* in a corner to cook. Firewood had to be purchased for cooking and water was fetched from a nearby well. All the groceries, *Jawar,* vegetables and sometimes non-veg like beef was unaffordable for us. The room had an open space in front. We bathed there in the open. At some distance, there was a public toilet maintained by the municipality with 5-6 seats in a row at a height, with damaged compartments, damaged roof on the top and open from the front. All the night excreta used to flow out from the back. It was dirty and unhygienic beyond imagination and tolerance. It stank unbearably and polluted all the surroundings at all times. The pigs wallowed in the filth. The *Bhangi* would come with a municipal tank to fill in the night soil. He would collect the excreta from each compartment from the back with an iron plate and collect it into a bucket and pour it into the wheeled van. People using the toilet would often drop shit on his hand and then he would abuse them from outside. Finally he would carry it to a long dumping open space and empty the van there. That would cause a further stink all around. Rainy seasons would be the worst. Even now when I write this, I feel that stinking smell in my nose and still I could almost vomit. There was a similar public toilet for women at a distance. Many would use the nearby open space closer to Maharwada early in the morning before sunrise to avoid all that.

It may be noted that there were many SC students from nearby villages all around staying on rent and going to schools and college. There was a boys' hostel nearby funded by the state welfare department, meant for SC-ST students run by a Mahar who was just literate. Intake was limited but criteria for admission were not fixed or known to people. The students used to get two meals and a place to sleep in a dormitory system. Known for discipline and cleanliness, the inmates woke up early in the morning to do the cleaning besides watering the garden plants. The manager was accused of manipulations and corruption. During vacations, the inmates had to vacate the hostel. There was no toilet facility in the hostel. The boys had to go to an open space early in the morning before sunrise. This hostel was located close to a stinking, huge, open drainage, carrying filth of the entire town. A part of Mahar basti was also closely located. The room where we shifted was close to the hostel and the Maharwada and the drainage. There was always a crowd of pigs fighting and making loud sounds with wet bodies from the flowing dirty black thick water from the drainage. They would always chase people going for open toilet. During and after the ritual, the pigs would run and rush to eat the excreta. I also had experienced this several times. The pigs were actually pets kept by the *Bhangis* as a source of income and also as the tradition of their community. They used to remove the pigs' hair and sell it besides using the excreta of the animals. And during special occasions like marriages, annual festival and treats for guests, they would catch the animal with very special tricks using a thick net. The animal used to make high pitched noises to escape. After cleaning it properly a *puja* was performed before killing the animal. After it was dead, they roasted it on fire and then cut it into pieces and then make a special delicacy from it. It was a prestige for them to treat any guest to this menu. Mahars abhorred this and considered it below their dignity to eat unhygienic and impure pork. Surprisingly, the Bhangis used to treat Mahars below them in all forms and practised untouchability with them. At the same time the Bhangis were averse to beef eating and hence maintained a distance from the Mahars.

However, the motivation and the spirit behind the education of these people in those days was worth appreciating. It was the tidal wave of Ambedkar's movement that built educational aspirations for these people. Many parents used to take loans or sell their land or belongings for the education of their children. However education for girls was still a distant development.

The school had almost all Brahmin and upper caste teachers and students. It was only for boys and uniforms were compulsory. The school also had a junior NCC wing that I joined. I completed two years of training and earned the Sergeant's rank. This helped me to be regular and self-disciplined. Here, all the teachers were very strict and good. Physical punishment was very common. However humiliation in the class in the presence of all the students over any mistake was also common. The English language teacher was very strict in particular. He taught English very well but used to beat students hard. For me it was very difficult to keep the school timings due to the distance between the school and our room; also it was difficult to meet daily needs like meals, fees and uniform expenses. I started working on daily wages with my cousin on the farms, cutting grass on holidays. Father used to help at times with some money, often by borrowing, collecting firewood from the village for cooking and sometimes even grains. I remember once he brought an old used shirt piece that was purchased from the weekly village bazaar. I was very thrilled and used it for many days. The studies were hard for me in the absence of any tuitions/classes or guidance and right through I only managed to pass on the border in every examination. But the most convenient and easy way out was not to study maths and science as I had chosen the Arts stream in the 9th standard.

My father had no money to pay my 10th standard exam fees. I vividly remember that one day I was very hungry and had nothing to eat. Finally I took out some solid black lentils and ate them and drank a glass of water. The hunger was gone. Then I sat for study. We were worried but finally father managed to find the money somehow. During these 3 years at the secondary level, I worked as a daily wager during the vacations on and off to support the family. The 10th exam was the board exam and was supposed to be tough to pass. Surprisingly I passed it with a good score of 59.5 per cent, narrowly missing the first class. But in those days this was considered a very high score. My elder brother was studying in the college and managing his study. He was getting a scholarship meant for SCs once in a year at the end.

In general I was considered to be a serious, studious and polite boy. As a student I was appreciated by everyone. However my mind was never at peace. I was disturbed, frustrated and despondent because of financial problems, family issues and the social inferiority complex. I would compare myself with rich-upper caste students, their clothes, language, the food they ate and the money they spent. I would feel inadequate, inferior and unworthy. I had no help and no sympathy. No outings, no entertainments, no special meals; except for beef at times as it was cheaper. In this state of mind, the most difficult task of reaching and passing the 10th standard was successfully fulfilled. All my mates from my village and of my caste had either dropped out or failed repeatedly and could not reach or clear SSC. The main secret of my success reaching and passing the 10th was that I never failed in between till that level. If I had failed even once, I would not have survived at all. The reasons being many fold: the expenses, no fees concession and becoming a target of social criticism. Of being labelled as a gone case.

5

Where Did My Voyage Take Me?

Higher Education: Trailblazing Education

The Milind College: With full joy and enthusiasm, my parents, my brother and myself decided that I should go to Aurangabad for higher studies. Many students from the SC community went there for studies mainly because the college gave a Government of India scholarship (post matric scholarship) amount per month in advance of the welfare department sanction of scholarship. This used to attract students from all over Maharashtra and quite a few of them also came from other states like Karnataka and Madhya Pradesh. The Milind College was established in 1950 by Babasaheb Ambedkar under the People's Education Society (PES). It was a college of preference for SC/ST students apart from the Siddhartha College of Arts and Science established in 1945 in Mumbai. The college at Aurangabad was very popular in those days and it was the only college in the Marathwada region that was under the Nizam's rule for about a century. It was an old and historical city established by Aurangzeb, and is well known for the Ellora and Ajanta caves in its vicinity. Within the city there is the famous Pawanchakki and Bibi ka Maqbara. Considering the importance and role of education, especially Higher Education, Babasaheb had started the colleges in the Marathwada region in particular with the help of his upper caste friends and activists like M.B. Chitnis and Tipnis (both Kayasthas) and others. Marathwada was known for its poor economy and social and educational backwardness with the highest SC population. There used to be record issues of caste-based atrocities in rural parts and severe practice of untouchability in the region. Babasaheb acquired some 150 acres of land from the Nizam with his personal influence for setting up the college. He named the college after the renowned Buddhist philosopher and monk Milind and the campus was named Nagsenvana. The college had Arts and Science streams. The college building architecture is very beautifully and meaningfully designed as per Buddhist architecture. The College gained name and fame very soon due to its high standards and its teaching staff. There were two huge hostels built for boys and one for girls. However, only a few SC students joined the college in those days. Most of the hostels used to be vacant, especially the ones for girls. Most of the teaching staff, from upper castes was chosen and appointed by Babasaheb himself. The students were also mainly from the upper castes. There was also a high school known as Milind Multipurpose High School in the same location. The distance between my village and the city of Aurangabad is an overnight journey by state transport bus. I used to travel for an hour by another bus to the district town Akola to catch the bus that went to Aurangabad.

The students after admission and verification of the certificates—necessarily the caste and income ones—would immediately receive an amount of Rs. 35 as scholarship advance. This would help students maintain the expenses for the entire month. The scholarship rate per month was Rs. 50 per month. The remaining balance would be reimbursed at the end after the annual examinations. They mostly stayed in rented rooms on a sharing basis all around the *bastis* that were mainly dominated by the Muslims and the SCs. Most of these people were economically very poor and the house rent used be a good source of income for them. Actually, the rooms would be cramped and unhygienic in congested localities; mostly newly made out of iron sheets. They would be with/without tap water, no toilet facility and mostly created with a space to bathe inside the rooms. Rooms with all these facilities would have a higher rent. Upper castes generally would not rent out such rooms to these students. They would stay and cook food on the kerosene stoves. If the owner of the house was Muslim and SC, they would cook beef. After passing the 10th board examination, one had to complete a one-year course known as the pre-university course (PUC) to join the degree course. However, those who did the 11th board examination would join the degree course directly. I joined the PUC and completed it in one year staying privately with my elder brother. Then he tried to put me in the government hostel meant for meritorious students from SC-ST and other communities. This was a special educational scheme run by the Maharashtra government for boys and girls in five major cities in the state including Aurangabad. These hostels were under a special scheme to promote education of meritorious students; hence they had all the facilities including meals, beds, local travel passes and instruments required for professional courses. Luckily I got admission in this hostel in the first year of my BA degree. This was in the midst of the academic year as there was one vacant seat as a student had left the hostel. I was very happy to stay there with so many facilities. The hostel was far away from the college. I had often to walk the distance as there was no direct city bus to reach the college.

On the way to college, I had to cross an old bridge that was on a *nallah* and the place was deserted. I used to get scared on this spot. Just a few days before the final examination, I was supposedly possessed by an evil spirit. It took a toll on my classes and studies. The hostel mates and the warden were all worried. There were some who ridiculed me and did not believe me and yet some others who tried to help. It affected my diet, sleep and eventually my health. Finally the warden wrote to my father about it and he came to take me back home. I went with him for treatment to take out the spirit from me through the service of a skilful magician. My elder brother by this time was working in a school near our village. Through him we discovered a man with the knowledge and skill of exorcising out the spirit. He was specially invited for my treatment. He performed all his rituals, black magic and all that to treat me. It took some days but I was finally cured and back to my old self. By then the exam had started in the college. I wanted to go and take the exam but everyone including my parents discouraged me. And thus I lost one academic year in my educational career. I also lost the hostel claim. I went back to Aurangabad to join college in the month of June. I took admission as a repeater. As a repeater, or once you fail at the exam you are not eligible for a scholarship. So I was not. However, the welfare department officer in the city advised me to apply after six months with a medical certificate which I did, and my scholarship was resettled.

The Classes: The college had both Science and Arts classes in the same building, hence it was always crowded. Arts classes used to be more crowded. The teachers were good. Most of the teachers were Brahmins. The Principal Mr. M.B. Chitnis was Babasaheb's associate in all his public and private activities including academic assistance. He was present and witness to mass conversion to Buddhism and himself converted along with Babasaheb. He was known to be a highly educated, intellectual and a committed follower of Babasaheb. He was an expert in Marathi literature. I am proud to say I was his student and he taught me modern Marathi literature. Mr. M.B. Chitnis and Dr. Gangadhar Pantawane were the leading teachers to start a monthly called *Ashmitadarsha*, a literary and intellectual magazine devoted to social causes. This group of teachers also really encouraged students to write their own lived experiences of life, poetry with social themes that were published in the magazine besides the college annual magazine. Slowly this gained respect and popularity in the social and literary field and proved to be responsible for the emergence of D*alit* literature in later years. Later Mr. Chitnis joined as Registrar of the Marathwada University and Dr. M.N. Wankhede, who was deputed by Babasaheb to study abroad, took over as principal. He was followed by Dr. Lokhande. Both were students of Milind College. It is noteworthy that most of the political leaders, social activists, poets, writers and teachers from the SC community today are products of that college and have been contributing to the cause of the community and society. However, the entire college community was dominated by the Mahars. The Mangs and Chambhars used to be relatively few in number and keep themselves away from the mainstream student community and other activities. There was a big auditorium built under the advice of Babasaheb known as *rangamancha* and all the cultural activities used to happen there.

However, during those days, the upper caste teachers started getting targeted by SC teachers and students, who accused them of being the oppressor Brahmins/upper castes and held them responsible for all the problems. A group of students used to quarrel and show disrespect to them by non-cooperation. This as reverse discrimination, led to a slow drop out of these teachers from the college and then getting replaced by SC teachers. The best teachers I had in this college were Dr. S.M. Pinge, Dr. V.K. Joshi. Dr. R.G. Jadhav, Dr. L.B. Raimane and Dr. Nathan. They all taught me till the BA level. Dr. V.V. Deshpande taught Sociology from the 11th standard till the MA at the university level. Classes used to be crowded. The teachers would follow only the lecture method. No asking/answering of questions and queries was encouraged. At the end of the academic year, the students went back home using the student public transport concession.

The college students were aware of their rights and had full awareness of social issues based on caste. Anything that would happen in the state related to SCs like atrocities-political or any other would cause the students to agitate, organize protests, morchas, etc. in very aggressive ways. This would invite anger, annoyance and disrespect to the cause by the city people. Frequently, local residents from upper castes would criticize the students blaming the college and the community. This would lead to losing the sympathy of those who were sympathetic to the cause.

However, it is so tragic to see that the college slowly lost its reputation. All the youth then started joining colleges run by different community trusts. These colleges were divided across the caste and community: Saraswati Bhuvan College would be generally preferred by Brhamins, Deogiri College by Marathas and Maulana Azad college by Muslims and so on. By now the PES had started a separate college of commerce naming it after Dr. Ambedkar. Most of the SC and ST students used to study at this college. This needs more elaboration considering the local politics in the city and region. Marathwada region has been dominated by rich Marathas and highly educated Brahmins. Next to Congress was the dominating Socialist party and its leadership led by Brahmins like Mr. Anant Bhalrao and Govind Bhai Saraf.

Both were known for their social and political values but the Milind college crowd would always criticize them as their views were interpreted as Brahminical and they would instead go by the Republican Party (RPI) ideology followed by the Dalit Panther Movement. This leadership used to be vocal, aggressive and often abusive and used to condemn Hinduism, and so on. This was supplemented by the newer issues in the college; discrimination and prejudice among those who belonged to Marathawada versus those from Vidarbha. The students-teachers from the Vidarbha region used to be in a majority. Known for their aggressiveness, they dominated the whole environment. The locals used to get agitated and protest against them. Of course there used to be provocation by teachers from both the sides plus the annoyance of upper caste people. All this led to the downfall of the college including falling academic standards. The same thing has happened to the colleges and schools in Mumbai and other places.

Today all the colleges run by the PES are functioning and running well. They also started an Engineering and Law College, but the number of students has gone down. One of the reasons could be the lack of giving scholarships on a monthly basis. However, overall enthusiasm and spirit is lost besides political crisis and infighting among the leadership and the groups across political lines in the absence of strong leadership. This reminds of the vision and mission in higher education strongly propounded by Babasaheb. I would describe this as one of the prominent reasons for the downfall of the political, social and educational movement of these communities in the state. Very few go in for higher education, fewer sustain it and very few succeed. Trained with poor quality of education and skills, despite reservations, we see fast growing and large-scale educated unemployment among these youth.

Despite all odds, I managed to survive and complete the BA degree clearing the examination every year. My elder brother in the meanwhile had joined his MA at the university. He completed two years but could not pass so he returned home to take up a teaching job at a private school close to our village. Being an untrained teacher he was probably paid a low salary. But he had no option. He worked there for two years and in the last year his services were terminated. Despite that he got married which added serious problems of money in the family. He was desperately looking for another job. But he did not get one. Finally he decided to go to Aurangabad and join LLB and keep trying for a job. He actually joined me with his newly-wed wife. We decided to stay together in a rented room. Brother, his wife (my Bhabhi) and I rented a room but had no source of income. Finally, Bhabhi joined the college with me and my brother joined LLB and survived financially for long on the scholarship amount we three got per month. In addition, I did some odd jobs to support ourselves. There was no question of any financial support from home.

Thus I earned my first degree: BA with second class. Bhabhi gave up education in between as she had a baby. She came from a rich family. Her father owned a huge amount of agricultural land but gave no support either way. My brother continued with the LLB. I decided to join MA Sociology in place of Marathi literature. I was good at both subjects, rather better in literature. However, the job being priority, I chose sociology as there was less demand for language and literature. Meanwhile, my younger brother joined us as he was not doing well in studies at our village. Parents used to visit us casually. It was literally a hand to mouth situation those days. Finally, my brother even had to mortgage my Bhabhi's gold jewellery.

Both parents used to work hard all the time and help us in all possible ways. Both of them were very proud of us, because we were good sons with all decency and courtesy and with no bad habits. Father used to go on telling proudly about our education to all who would hear: the neighbors, community people, the villagers and even at weddings! Upper caste people also were appreciative and some of them were forthcoming with monetary help on occasions. Many of our caste fellows were jealous of us as none of their children continued with their education.

Joined Masters: After passing undergraduation at the college, most of the students would join postgraduation in their respective subjects at the university of Marathwada. The university is located close to the college and at the base of barren hills that have oldest Buddhist caves. Even older than Ajanta and Ellora caves. A few of them would join some jobs out of real need and give up education. The university campus had a huge piece of land with partially cultivable and mostly barren land. Surrounding areas were populated by Muslim, Dalit and non-Dalit communities with physical divisions of *bastis*. Many of them lost their ancestral houses and land to the university. Babasaheb had created the background to start this university along with local elite people.

I joined MA Sociology in 1972. The Department of Sociology was very popular for its liberal and fair treatment to the SC students as compared to the other departments. It was more so because of Dr. Sudha Kaldate, wife of Bapu Kaldate who was Socialist by political/ideological orientation and an activist/social worker who used to preach and practice equality. They had an inter-caste marriage, he was a Maratha and she was a Brahmin from Pune coming from a prestigious family. Kaldate was a staunch political leader, a good orator and a highly respected person. But his voice was stifled due to the strong hold of the Congress Party and its leadership dominated by the Marathas. Besides Dr. Sudha Kaldate, the department had Prof. M.G. Kulkarni, student of Prof. Ghurey, liberal of attitude and two more faculty members. The department office had a steno-typist and a junior clerk who was a young lady. Both were Brahmins and very caste conscious. They treated SC students badly and even ridiculed them. The other departments' majority faculty would be either Brahmins or Marathas. Mostly biased against SCs and often the SC students used to face social and academic discrimination directly or indirectly. Among the students, Marathas and Brahmins used to be the majority. There were always social tensions and quarrels between the Maratha students and the SC students over all kinds of issues including student elections.

Most of the SC students had financial problems. Here they were getting their scholarships only once at the end of final examinations, unlike Milind College on a monthly basis. Somehow they used to manage by doing some odd jobs. I was in the same condition but at least used to get daily meals because of my brother and his family. I saw many students going hungry due to lack of money. The overall environment was not conducive for social and academic discourse on the campus. There was always rivalry between the SCs and Non-SCs over Ambedkar and his ideology, caste and reservation policy, etc. Those days at the postgraduation level the medium of teaching was only English. This was a major problem for everyone but more so for the SC students and they would have problems in learning, comprehending the classes and reading books in the library, as most of them came from a vernacular background. I had similar problems; although slightly better in English language than others. This was the last batch of the English medium. After a long agitation by the students, the university introduced the Marathi medium. This used to affect their academic performance besides bringing out psychological problems of inferiority and mental blocks. We had to do four courses a year, so eight in a period of two years for the MA. In the classes, Dr. Sudha Kaldate used to come to the department and classes with sleeveless clothes. Those days very few women wore such clothes. It was considered to be a sign of a modern and progressive lifestyle. However, it used to be a big problem for me initially. I used to feel very shy by her appearance in class and around the department and used to put my head down and not to open my mouth in the class. But she was a good teacher and a decent person. I slowly settled down and started interacting with her. This was the first time in my life that I saw a woman wearing sleeveless outfits.

The teachers at the Sociology department were competent and well-qualified; they would complete all the courses on time. The only exam, the annual exam, took place at the end of the year. Here too, I managed to complete the first year, with many difficulties like procuring books, clothes to wear, money, etc. The family's financial burden was only managed by the scholarship that my brother and his wife received. Often we could not pay the monthly rent. At times we had nothing to eat, not even firewood for cooking. Luckily, there was a government medical college hospital nearby and we could depend on free medical treatment from this hospital, for treatment of all our major or minor ailments. Once a very funny incident happened over the issue of drought in that region in 1971. People from around Aurangabad, would come to the hospital for medical treatment and stay on a rental basis around the hospital. The room we were staying in belonged to an upper caste person but all the tenants living in different rooms were SCs. But the locality had a majority Muslim population. A lady from a nearby village rented a room opposite ours, owned by a Muslim for a month or so for her mother's treatment of tuberculosis. They belonged to the Maratha caste, always showing pride and superiority in everything. They often interacted and borrowed things from us. They did not know our caste. One fine day when I came back from my classes this lady started chatting with me. She told me the reasons behind the severe drought that occurred that year. Ironically, that day we had studied the caste system in India, in the sociology class. And here was this lady very confidently and regretfully narrating the reasons behind the drought: because people no longer practised the caste system and untouchability which was the creation of God. She and her ailing mother were illiterate and typical villagers. I kept listening to her but could not explain or narrate to her as to why drought occurred and that caste and untouchability had nothing to do with that. What was taught in the sociology class was just not meaningful or adequate to explain to her and I just could not summon up the courage to explain or argue with her probably because I was so conscious of my caste. She was a Maratha, the dominant caste in the region. It would have been futile to make her understand; it was beyond her capacity to learn and beyond my capacity to teach or correct.

The room we rented was one among the six rooms divided in two rows opposite to each other. All the tenants were living on a rental basis and belonged to the SC community except one upper caste (Dhangar, now under OBC) family with all kinds of caste and religious orthodoxy. They maintained proper distance from all the SC families and never used to inter dine or share food or other things. However, the locality was known to be a Muslim locality.

Most of them were very poor and engaged in many odd occupations. The locality was congested, over populated and filthy with dust and garbage. Many houses had open toilets covered with plastic or gunny bag sheets with doors made of wood or thick sheets. The drainage water and the toilet shit used to flow all around and often stagnate. The *bhangi* (from the north) would every morning go to each house and pour water into the toilets to clean them. This would always stink and pollute the air. On the whole it was very unhygienic. Our rooms had similar toilets but with proper tin sheds and wooden doors. But cleaning the toilets was the same as the others. I think it is a matter of routine and getting used to. I remember thinking that we were better off than many others. The local SCs were in a pathetic condition. Their dependence on upper castes and Muslims was very high. Gross unawareness, illiteracy, poverty and untouchability were the major problems faced by them. The local SC youths remained uneducated except for a few who reached the secondary level. On the other hand, all the college going students in the vicinity of Milind College used to come to study from all over Maharashtra and stay in the SC localities. It was noteworthy to see the enthusiasm for education among these youths. During the exam preparations the library used to be crowded and it was actually an impediment for concentration. Many students, including me, used to go out in the open spaces around the campus under trees to study. The rooms were small and full of heat with iron sheets, so sitting outside in the fresh air was actually better. Again, I would call this a tidal wave of social and educational movement that was started by Babasaheb. Thousands of students graduated every year despite all the social and financial odds. The city of Aurangabad and Milind College were considered to be the centre of a spirited educational and social-political movement. This has contributed in a big way to the community in general and to Babasaheb's mission. I feel proud and owe so much to this college that laid the foundations of my educational career and social awareness along with developing self-respect.

So I got into the MA second year. The university level education, the environment, the enthusiasm to learn and social life were all rather thrilling experiences for me. I look back and realize that it added to my confidence, self-respect and knowledge. However, when it came to money and making ends meet, there was plenty of tension and discouragement. Still, I managed to soldier on and completed the MA first year. Regular attendance in the classes and regular use of the library helped me pass the examination; although there were problems in understanding the subject and reading books in English. After the results were declared, we all went to our village on vacation for a few days. After coming back, I started looking for a job in order to support ourselves. After the new academic year began, the university and the department started evening classes for sociology final year. This was a great opportunity for me. I shifted to evening classes. The timing was 6.30 pm to 9.30 pm. We were seven students. I applied for the post-matric scholarship with others. That was to be given only at the end of the academic year. I met the Registrar and requested him to help me by releasing an advance from the scholarship to learn auto rickshaw driving for earning some money. He was very happy to know that I chose to work and earn during studies but was not willing to give an advance. With several requests and insistence, however, he sanctioned Rs. 100. I felt very grateful to him. I paid Rs. 60 to a known auto driver to train me. He taught me driving for five-six days and then refused to teach under some or the other pretext. Luckily the department of small-scale industries, government of Maharashtra, in those days undertook an all Maharashtra census of small-scale industries in the state. The director of this office in Aurangabad city announced posts of enumerators. I got to know of this through friends. I appeared for the interview on the given dates with many others. I was fortunate enough to get selected. We were to get local travel fare and a reasonable amount as salary for three months. The job was to visit such industry housed/ offices in and around the city in a group and fill up the structured questionnaire. This job got extended for another two months as it was not completed in the given time. We were given a fixed target of covering the units. Tiring and exhausting as it was, I enjoyed it because of the earnings. After working for the full day, I would go and attend classes in the evening. This gave me and my brother quite a relief from financial worries. After this job was over and after a gap of one-two months, I did examination supervision after finishing my MA final year exam. I got this work through the Deputy Registrar of Exams whom I met personally and managed to persuade. He gave me the job that continued for ten days. I earned a substantial amount of money out of this. This was followed by the odd job of filling up mark sheets of the students who wrote exams. This lasted for about a week which also helped us a lot financially. At the final MA exam one of our course papers was Social Science Research Methods that was taught by an excellent teacher. But many others and I, found it difficult to understand the subject in addition to the English language and the technical/statistical contents. On the morning of the day I was to write the paper, I was in the library trying to read and somehow not understand the topics. At the end I got very agitated. I left the reading room and came to the main entry gate where the library check desk was located.

A lady on duty saw me with tears in my eyes. She called me and gave me some soothing words of encouragement and support, saying that since I had been a regular and hard working student, I would pass. She told me not to worry. My spirits rose with this emotional support and encouragement. I wrote the paper that noon. It was well done. When the results came out, I was surprised to see that I had scored the highest marks in that paper as against the one I was very confident about, industrial sociology. Thus with against all odds I completed my MA degree in sociology with 55.5 per cent marks. I was very happy and excited mainly because I was the first postgraduate not only in my family but also in my village and all the surrounding villages. My MA days saw a deep hurting and humiliating incident of caste-based discrimination and untouchability. Once I went to a Brahmin lady professor's residence for a signature. It was hot summer. I felt thirsty so I asked the professor's old mother for a glass of water as the professor was not there. She gave me water to drink with reluctance but in a tumbler that was used for cleaning the courtyard with a lot of dust and filth around the tumbler. I took it but did not drink the water and left the place.

In the meantime, mother joined us in Aurangabad for her treatment of *nasur* (fistula) that had been there for several years. The wound was on the face between the right eyebrow and the upper eyelid. This began with a small boil that was treated with local medicines but did not work. The tiny hole would always flow with pus. Father did not pay serious attention to her problem. Neither did he know how to go ahead with treatment nor did he have money.

At the home front in Aurangabad, Bhabhi went to college for two years but did not show much interest in studies. Her main purpose in attending the college was the scholarship. After she conceived, I had to drop her at her parents' village for delivery and return to Aurangabad. Meanwhile, my younger brother passed his 8th exam and went back home. My elder brother was still pursuing law and looking for a job. In Bhabhi's absence, I had to cook and do everything in the house. For that matter, my brother never did any major or minor domestic work; neither here nor at the village. I would always share the domestic work with my mother since childhood and continued even after Bhabhi joined us and still continue to do so in some way or the other after marriage.

After the MA results, it was a serious matter to decide as to what to do next. Getting a job was top priority. But only an MA degree would not fetch one a job even in those days. Joining PhD was out of the question. Finally we jointly decided that I should join the BEd degree course as that could easily translate into a job. So I applied at the Government College of Education for the BEd course and got the admission out of the reserved quota. The fees were reasonable for the SCs. I paid the fees but could not attend classes as mother was admitted for treatment in the government hospital. I met the principal and explained the problem to her. She allowed me to tend to my mother for a week. Mother underwent surgery, and I continued to care for her, along with my brother occasionally. The BEd was a professional degree and attendance was observed very strictly. Besides, there was a lot of homework and other academic engagements. All the teachers were Brahmins. They were in charge of the internal assessments, including giving marks for practical teaching lessons. So everybody was scared of them. We SC students more so because the teachers were perceived to be biased against our caste. Added to this pressure was the gruelling everyday schedule: I had to walk a long distance from home to the college generally with no money. During breaks in the college, I used to skip snack and tea and remain away from those who would have it. Teaching lessons in different schools used to be even more problematic since I had to travel on foot. The scholarship was due only at the end of the year. Somehow I managed. However, I took part in different extracurricular activities like debates, discussions on various issues, and the annual function. Thus with great pressure and problems, I completed this one year course and passed with a second class, which was considered as poor performance. First class and above were considered to be a good performance at BEd. Anyway, it was a rare and rewarding opportunity and quite an achievement at personal and social levels that added to my prestige and life achievements.

My elder brother got a job as a clerk in the district magistrate's office unexpectedly. This was a job on a temporary basis against the positions vacated due to the long strike by government employees of the state. The temporary employees were recruited as a strategy to break the strike. It went on for a few months which helped us financially. He continued in the job even after the strike was over for the period that counted for making him a regular employee as per the law. As a result, he was given a posting in the PWD (then known as B & C) department as a clerk in Aurangabad itself. By then, he had completed his law and cleared his MA with me after five attempts. This qualification was considered very high for the post for which he was interviewed at the PWD department. He got selected and joined there. This was an assured source of regular financial income that gave real relief to all of us. In the meantime, I went back to the village to bring Bhabhi back to Aurangabad; she by then had delivered a baby boy. I got the younger brother and Bhabhi back. Mother by then was in better health after surgery.

Vocation or Avocation?—Pathway to Success

The First Job: Now it was my turn to take up a job after completing my MA and BEd. The best opportunity was to take up a teaching job at high school level. There were many advertisements by such schools. I applied to four schools and was called for the personal interview at all four. I appeared for two of them and got selected in both. I chose to join Rashtriya Hindi Vidyalaya Junior College (+2 level) at Jalna; some 150 kilometres away from Aurangabad; a town known as a business centre in the area. This high school was established by Marwari businessmen. All the trustees and most of the teachers belonged to Brahmin and Marwari communities who had settled in the town. Exceptionally, there was one SC teacher (physical training) who used to be harassed and always troubled by everyone. The junior college was attached to the high school that was old and reputed. It was also the first batch of the college. I was to teach sociology as my appointment was at the 11th standard. This school was a Hindi medium school and I was supposed to teach sociology through English and Hindi. After a week or so, the 11th standard was closed by the school due to lack of the required number of students to run the class. Then I was absorbed at the secondary level and started teaching Marathi, English, Civics and History from the 5th to 7th standard. It took me three months to receive my salary because the post required sanction from the education department. I was literally without money. I often took loans against interest from fellow teachers who used to lend money on a regular basis. Most of them were Marwaris. Accommodation was a major problem as I did not have money to rent a room and the Marwaris or the local upper caste people would not rent out a room to me. One teacher teaching at primary level of the same school was staying in a rented small room owned by a Marwari.

His surname was the same as mine. I requested him to accommodate me. He agreed and I started staying with him. The next issue was meals. For many days he allowed me to cook and eat with him at his cost. After a few days he started taunting me over the meals and money. I used to coolly listen to him, being helpless. My hopes were from the salary I expected to receive. Slowly I came to know from somebody that he was an orphan brought up and educated by a Christian missionary. He never revealed this to anyone but used to identify with the SC community. This may be the reason why he assisted me. It was an immense help to me and I still owe him so much. After receiving my three months salary, I shifted to a separate rented room, paid my debts and also paid all the other pending dues at Aurangabad including the room rent to the landlord there.

When the year ended, my elder brother was transferred to Nanded on promotion as storekeeper. Before joining me at Jalna, I did all the shifting work of carrying belongings by train and immediately rushed to bring Bhabhi to Nanded. By this time I had completed one academic year as a teacher at Jalna. Being on probation, the school authorities refused to confirm my job. Despite several persuasions, I was not given continuation. I was jobless and did not know what to do. My brother told me to apply for a job again. But I had a strong inner will to study further. Somehow I found a way out. I was in touch with an SC friend Shrikant, who hailed from Karnataka and studied BA at Milind College and MA at the university with me. After his MA, he went to JNU (Jawaharlal Nehru University, New Delhi) for his PhD. I wrote to him and he advised me to join JNU like him. His source of inspiration was Prof. S. Thorat who was also a student of Milind College and later taught at the same college before going to JNU as a fellow teacher. Prof. Thorat followed Prof. Mandavdhare who was also teaching at Milind College and joined JNU for his PhD as a fellow teacher. Thus, after Prof. Thorat, many of the students who studied at Milind College joined JNU, encouraging and inspiring each other. Finally I decided on my own to try and apply for the MPhil/PhD course at JNU. My brother was against it. The friend sent me an application form that I did not even know how to fill up fully and correctly. I went to the teacher who taught me at MA for help. He kindly helped me fill in the application, which I duly posted. The major source of inspiration and motivation was the reimbursement of travel both ways.

The JNU Days: The Jawaharlal Nehru University (JNU) had brought a real change in my life; both academically and socially. I applied for the MPhil/PhD integrated course at the two centres—Zakir Husain Centre for Educational Studies and Social System Studies (both under the School of Social Sciences). In June I received the call from JNU telegraphically to appear for the entrance exam and personal interview. I was determined to leave for Delhi and my brother was opposing it. Ultimately, a week before the interview dates I packed my things with one suitcase, one handbag and a mattress. I was totally unaware of train travel for such a long distance and the possible difficulties during the journey. One fine noon while my brother was at work, I bid goodbye to Bhabhi and the child and went to the Nanded railway station. I had no seat reservations nor tickets. I purchased running tickets for New Delhi. The trains that go to New Delhi run on the main line—Bombay—Delhi via Manmad junction. From Nanded to Manmad it took six-seven hours to reach. It was a narrow gauge single line and the train would stop at every station. At the Nanded station while waiting for the arrival of the train a Sikh gentleman (Nanded is one important pilgrimage of Sikhs) guided me and gave me a lot of courage to travel. He was very happy to see me going to Delhi for studies but was ridiculing me for travelling with no reservation and with a mattress. Actually he was right, but he did not know I was carrying the mattress to save money so that I did not have to spend on it in Delhi. I got to know from the Sardarji that the train that was available to Delhi was the Punjab Mail that arrives at Manmad at 9.30 pm from Bombay. The metre gauge train arrived at Nanded from Secundarabad. I boarded the general coach with all my things. It goes without saying that it was a crowded coach. I managed to get a seat. It was June, month of high heat. I could not afford to buy cold drinks, tea or food on the way. I got off the train almost every third station to quench my thirst. There were many Sikhs travelling in the coach after they completed their pilgrimage. They shared their food with me after they enquired about me and the purpose of my journey. At last we reached Manmad at about an hour before the Punjab mail arrived. After enquiry, I reached the platform where the train would arrive. It was so difficult to carry the bag, the mattress and the suitcase from over the bridge. Feeling very hungry, I ate something that was the cheapest. The train arrived half an hour late. I requested the TT for a berth. It was not available. Then requested him to allow me to enter the coach which he bluntly refused. The train started moving slowly. Finally I literally threw the luggage into the ladies coach and got in. The ladies started shouting at me, asking me to get down. I requested them very humbly to allow me to travel till the next station. They agreed. At the next station, I threw out the luggage and got off the ladies' coach. I requested the coolie (porter) to help me get into the general coach with my belongings. He agreed and asked for Rs.4 to do that. The coach was over crowded and was not possible to get in through the entry gate. The coolie literally lifted me and pushed me into the coach through the window followed by my luggage. This could happen through the window because those days the trains had windows without bars. I struggled to get a place to sit but in vain. It was already very crowded and passengers were fighting for seats. Somehow I managed to keep my baggage under the seat. I was standing on one leg with barely any space to move. The train again started late. It was about 11 pm. I was feeling hungry but I had no space to move; also, I was afraid to lose even that space if I got down for food. One of my co-passengers gave me water to drink. That's all! One whole night of no sleep, no seat, no food and just standing on one leg till the next day late morning. At Gwalior, it was a relief to finally get some space to sit. Here two youths boarded the coach, brother and sister. One of the passengers started misbehaving with the girl. Finally it resulted in verbal fights. Others finally intervened and resolved the quarrel. The girl was so scared. Now it was day time with very hot unbearable winds flowing in through the windows. I was curious to see the stations. It was my first experience of a long journey, which was thrilling. I managed to eat something hurriedly at Jhansi station. Towards the end of the day our train reached Agra. I was astonished to see the station and imagined the Taj Mahal considering myself to be lucky to have come this far. Finally the train arrived at New Delhi station at about 10 pm; much later than the scheduled time. Delhi was very hot and humid even at that hour of night. I got down at the station with luggage and felt completely lost. Telling myself not to lose courage, I decided to keep the luggage in the cloak room. After reaching the cloak room, I realized they needed to lock the bag which I did not have. Requesting the man there, I rushed out of the station and fortunately found a shop open. I purchased a lock and went back running and locked the bag and handed it over to the person. I got a receipt and again came out of the station. I tried to call the JNU friend from a public booth but did not succeed. After enquiring, I walked down for ten minutes and got the city bus to reach JNU. Again, luck favoured me. Everything was unfamiliar and new: the city, the station, the weather, the language people spoke. I was not comfortable in spoken Hindi and English in those days. The bus dropped me at the then old campus of JNU, close to Munirka. The hostels were located in the new campus so I had to walk down for nearly half an hour to the new campus. After entering the new campus, I was guided by someone to the Kamal complex where luckily I found my friend and two more whom I knew since the Aurangabad days. I felt so happy and relieved. I chatted and had some snacks, tea and bread. After some time we went to the hostel where my friend was staying. I spent the night in his room. The next morning my friend took me around the whole campus. I was so happy and thrilled to see such a huge campus—big buildings built with pink open bricks walls. The hostels had single room accommodation for students. Teachers had fancy independent quarters. Girls were walking and mixing with boys so freely. Everybody was speaking fluent English with a Westernized accent. The male-female proximity, their boldness and openness was surprising and unfamiliar to me. This was the first time in my life that I got to see such a free environment that crossed all barriers of gender, caste, language and region, rich and poor. It was confusing and disconcerting, making me shy and withdrawn sometimes. To reply to an introduction used to be difficult for me due to hesitation and the language problem. I used to think this was England and not India. After settling down, I wrote all about the JNU environment to my brother saying it was London not Delhi; although I had never seen London then. I felt most fortunate to have come here but at the same time felt inferior and anxious about whether I would be able to cope and study.

After three-four days I sat for the entrance test. Prof. Karuna Chanana was the exam supervisor who was my research supervisor later. I answered the question, “Is sociology a science and why?”, common to both the centres for admission. The next day followed with a personal interview for the Zakir Husain Centre. Prof. Tapas Majumdar was in the chair with three more lady faculty members including Prof. Chanana. When my turn came, I was nervous and scared owing to lack of English language skills. Luckily they asked questions related to educational problems and the topic of my research interest. I answered the questions, perhaps to their satisfaction. All of them were informal, pleasant and encouraging. This was a new experience for me as my prior university experience with teachers was different: always keeping a distance, talking mechanically using a harsh and strict tone. The following morning with the advice of my friends, I went to the teachers at the centre and asked about my results giving reasons for being unable to stay longer because of the financial crunch. I was informally told that I was selected for the course with the condition of not revealing to anyone. I was very happy! My dream of studying at JNU and earning the research degree had come true. I then went to the accounts section to claim my travel expenses which I got easily. The day after that I had an interview at the Centre for the Study of Social System but I did not appear because I was more interested in the education field perhaps due to my BEd degree and the teaching experience. I was given a room to stay in Sutlej Hostel on a temporary basis till the admission process got over. All the new aspiring students were given such accommodation.

After that my friend, Shrikant and I went around Delhi

visiting different places and also went to watch a movie. The friend was my guide. This took some amount to spend money for travel, food and the movie. In addition, I paid for the room and also had to pay for three meals everyday; although at a quite reasonable cost. Somehow, I did not realize that I was exhausting the limited money I had. At the time of paying fees for admission and hostel deposit, I realized it and was only left with a small amount which was not sufficient. Since there was a gap of a few days to start the classes, I wanted to go back home and come again to the university with some money. Due to the shortage of money, I cancelled the plan. All the other familiar Maharashtrian friends who came from Aurangabad were in the same condition so no one could lend me the money. It was not possible to ask my brother for money as he had joined his job recently and was still to receive his salary. But I requested him to send some and he sent an amount by telegraphic money order. That helped to sustain me for a few days. After that also I depended on borrowing money from friends and my brother. The academic session began. In all, we were 12 students for the MPhil courses admitted from different disciplines of economics, sociology, psychology and history to study education. I was pleasantly surprised to see the openness, informality and friendliness of the teachers interacting respectfully with students. One could meet, talk and ask them for anything even out of the academic sphere. Any student could meet the teacher any time and they would welcome us and offer a seat. This was a new thing for me since no teacher so far had welcomed and offered a seat. The students also used to go and meet the teachers at their houses on the campus. Some of them also held classes in their homes. This was the situation in the entire university campus both in academics and administration. There was no difference and distance between male and female. Everybody would maintain the expected respect and equality. In the classes it was a free atmosphere. Question-answer sessions and disagreements were common practice. I wish all the universities had these practices. My problem was more in adjusting to such a new (although positive and conducive for learning and growing academically) culture. In the classes I felt shy, reluctant and inferior first due to language difficulties and owing to the accent of the others including teachers and second by the entire western lifestyle, mannerisms and expressions. Many students including some girls used to smoke openly. This was very strange and a shocking thing for me to observe. However, this did not mean that there was no respect among and between them. After a semester, we were allotted supervisors according to our respective disciplines. As I was from a sociology background, the sociology faculty supervisor was allotted to me with another student Geetha Nambissan and the supervisor was Dr. Karuna Chanana. Geetha was not only a fellow-student but also a guide in many ways especially when I struggled with the English language. She continues to be a close friend and confidante, always encouraging my efforts with empathy and sensitivity. The Zakir Husain Centre located in the old campus was relatively small with educational approach to four major disciplines like economics, sociology, psychology and history. It had four-five faculty members and hardly 20-25 students including seniors.

The extreme Delhi climate was a major problem especially for those coming from the South. I found it very difficult to face the extreme cold and heat. I fell sick frequently. One winter evening I went to Connaught Place alone just to see things around. By the time I got ready to go back it was dark. The weather was chilly and windy. I went to the bus stop opposite Hotel Janpath. It was the only bus route (615) to the JNU campus. But I was waiting in the opposite direction and got confused. It was getting late and darker. There were two-three persons waiting for the bus. The roads were deserted. Finally I asked the young boys about the bus and the direction. First they laughed at me and then told me to go to the other direction. I told them about myself and expressed my despair. Finally I got the bus. By the time I reached the new campus, the mess was closed. Then I had to eat outside at the *dhaba* spending more money.

At that time the number of schools and courses offered were limited, so everyone used to get an independent room in the hostels. I was allotted a room in Sutlej Hostel at the beginning during the admission procedure and after admission I continued to stay in the same room (341) till I left JNU. This is where I first met the warden of Sutlej Hostel Dr. Nandu Ram. He was the first SC faculty in JNU and was known to always interact with and encourege students from marginalized communities. The students in the hostel were cooperative, understanding and open to discussing issues and helping each other. They were from all over the country representing the South, North, East and West India. English was the language of communication. Those days Hindi was hardly used for communication. In spite of my language difficulties, I was accepted and encouraged. The environment was such that locking the room while going out was not considered necessary. I do not remember hearing any incident of loss of valuables or any theft.

Open discussions, debates, arguments, counter arguments and disagreements were common and special features of the academic and social life in JNU. The teachers were open to such interaction and always encouraged discussions in the classes and outside. The topics and issues could be anything like academics, politics: national and international, economy, culture, religion and other social issues. The discussions would begin from morning at the breakfast table and go on till late at night in the *dhabas*. This would add to knowledge, awareness and build up confidence besides learning argumentative skills and logical understanding. JNU from the beginning has been a hub of party politics with different ideological orientations and commitments. It has been mainly known for and dominated by the communist party politics like the CPI (Communist Party of India) and CPM (Communist Party of India (Marxist) with their student wings like AISF (All India Students' Federation) and SFI (Students' Federation of India). Yet there was a third force among the students called Free Thinkers. The free thinkers had political orientation with no support or favour to any particular party. A few student followers of the National Congress used to sit silently on the back benches. ABVP (Akhil Bharatiya Vidyarthi Parishad) was totally absent in JNU those days. All the other student wings of political parties now in the limelight are the development of later times. Many faculty members also were openly or/and silently the party members or the card holders or sympathizers of the political parties. The students used to organize lectures in the mess of different hostels late in the evening after dinner. All types of personalities like politicians, activists, academicians, artists and journalists at national and international level used to come and deliver lectures on the topics of relevance followed by discussions and question-answer sessions. I was fortunate to attend lectures by a Nobel Prize winning lady economist from the USA and Mr. Willy Brandt who was Chancellor of West Germany. All this added to my rich experience, knowledge and confidence: academically, socially and intellectually. Almost all national level party leaders, ministers and members of Parliament used to be in touch with JNU student leaders. Such an open, democratic and intellectually motivating environment makes a great difference to the society and I wish all the universities would follow this tradition.

The SC-ST students who were admitted through the reservation quota had their formal and informal groups. They used to meet formally and informally to discuss their academic, social and political problems. The SCs from Maharashtra used to be in front and take the lead. Discussions on Dr. Ambedkar's life, his political ideology, his contributions to the nation and the Dalits, reservations, etc. used to be the core issues of discourse. The ST students from the north-east, and other parts of the country who were unaware of him used to show reluctance and be passive over the issues. But slowly they understood and were convinced about Dr. Ambedkar and his role in the country. However, these students were divided on political lines. Some were in support of the left party ideology; particularly the SFI because they dominated the political scenario. The others were fully in support of Ambedkar and his ideology and a few were also neutral. They also had the Ambedkar Study Circle engaged in organizing lectures and discussions on Dalit issues.

The overall situation was that Ambedkar and the issues of SC-ST would get ignored by all the parties including the left. Caste, untouchability and all related issues including the atrocities, exploitation and suppression by the upper castes in the country were issues that were rarely discussed with understanding. They used to argue that once the revolution occurs, all the issues will automatically be resolved. Most of these student leaders belonged to upper castes coming from privileged backgrounds and belonged to 2nd, 3rd or 4th

generation learners mostly with English education. Their language, appearance, culture, lifestyle, soft skills, etc. were Westernized, urbanized and elitist. Although they talked of the layman, common masses, equality, revolution and change, they were very far from the actual experience of a layman. We SC students would question, argue and discuss all these issues with them. Sitaram Yechuri, the popular CPM leader was my hostel mate pursuing his Masters. As a student leader he was popular and a convincing speaker. There were many others like him but from the upper caste and middle class background. This would create a politically negative impact on our minds and perceptions. We could not identify with them and accept them as our leaders. Their class analysis of the world and Indian society was found to be full of jargon and above the ground realities. Their ideals used to be derived from the then USSR, China and Cuba with the communist frame of ideology completely unsuited and irrelevant to our society. Even today the situation remains the same. I personally have had serious discussions with many student leaders over these issues but they have been fruitless. For many such student leaders it used to be a training and learning ground for political leadership at the national level and therefore perhaps we see many such JNU products today at national level politics from different parties. Devi Prasad Tripathi, Digvijay Singh, Sitaram Yechuri, Prakash Karat, Ranjana Kumari and Sanjana Kumari (sisters) and Ramesh Dixtit, are some examples. In fact, the political rivalry was mainly between the three ideological paths: the two left parties, i.e. CPM and CPI, and the Socialist group with the ideal of Dr. Ram Manohar Lohia. I was myself inclined more towards the Socialist group as they addressed the social issues of caste and untouchability, but I never subscribed to communist ideas.

I joined JNU during the emergency in 1977. Some of these student leaders were arrested and jailed for several months. Jasbir Singh, a Sikh SC from Punjab was badly tortured in the jail. He was a follower and activist of the Lohiya ideology. Almost all the JNU students and teachers were against the emergency. I myself hardly felt the difference under the emergency; may be because I did not know the meaning or seriousness of it. One thing was beyond my understanding about all these students and their political activism, and that was how they could afford time and money and how they could study while being engaged in full time politics. However, despite all the contradictions and political activism and differences, JNU always proved to be productive socially, politically, academically and intellectually. It produced all types of personalities at national level and also at international level such as diplomats, academicians, civil servants, police officers, writers, etc. Yet a few of them spoiled their lives and careers due to excessive politics; they could not complete their studies. In the case of SC-ST students, most of them being first generation learners and from vernacular backgrounds faced language problems compounded with issues like no research/analytical abilities and lack of proper guidance and motivation. Their academic performance was average and many of them were unable to complete their research work on time. I saw many of them dropping out of the course towards the end. Most of them were in need of an income, and they took up jobs and left JNU without a degree. One may call it a waste of resources or academic waste. However, given the circumstances, some extra efforts like personal attention, proper guidance, some remedial courses with sympathetic approach could have saved their anspirations and academic stagnation. The TISS experiment of this kind has yielded very positive results in such cases. This experiment will be shared and discussed in detail in subsequent chapters.

The experiences and problems I faced at JNU could be categorized in three major ways: 1. The cultural shock I suffered. 2. The language problem and 3. The academic one, in terms of inability to understand and comprehend the concepts, ideas, issues and knowledge of the subject(s). It could have depended on the teachers, their teaching skills and the attitude towards students like me. Also I attribute my weaknesses to the poor academic training that was received till my Masters. I am sure the teachers' sensitivity in such circumstances matters a lot; particularly for those who come from multiple handicapped backgrounds besides the social stigma of caste/tribe. However, I would still place the JNU environment as much better and more positive than any other university in the country. My academic survival in JNU has been a big surprise. I consider it as the struggle that had several dimensions. My teachers at in the MPhil course were genuine and sympathetic teachers. I must mention here Prof. Tapas Majumdar and Prof. Karuna Chanana in particular for their encouragement and good teaching skills. After completing two semesters of course work, all the students were allotted supervisors according to the disciplines. My initial interest was to do research on the school dropout problem among the SC students. However, there were already many studies on the topic, so I was advised to think of some new area. After discussions, I decided to work on occupational mobility among the SC graduates. It interested me because I was very curious to know what exactly these graduates are doing after they completed graduation in 1972 from the Milind College, Aurangabad and especially those who were my classmates at the College. It was empirically relevant to know their occupational status being graduate, SC with reservations and having studied in the college where they had every opportunity to develop. The study was for MPhil dissertation based on primary data. To my surprise, most of the sampled respondents were either unemployed or under employed during the years 1972 to 1978. Those employed were working at lower level government jobs. The unemployed ones were doing some odd private jobs and yet a few were working as labourers. Such a situation could cause an alarm when we talked of education, change, mobility and development of weaker sections besides various programmes for their upliftment. Who was to blame for this situation? The education system, the government, the policies, the graduates themselves or the society itself? What could be their mindset, with feelings of guilt being graduates? What must they be telling their parents about such a situation? I had been lucky to complete postgraduation and a professional degree and do a job for a year and then opt for research degrees. If compared with today's situation, I would not see much of a difference and that is due to the cut throat competition in education and employment. The private sector that demands quality and performance along with increasing bias about the caste status and the reservation policy, wherein the government is slowly withdrawing from education and employment sectors.

At JNU I could survive financially because I was sanctioned a research fellowship from both ICSSR (Indian Council of Social Science Research) and the UGC (University Grants Commission). I chose to accept the UGC one. Those days during vacations I used to visit my parents at home in the village and brothers at Nanded where they were working. I only bought selected things for loved ones to avoid extra expenses. Sometimes I gave/sent money to my parents. Everyone in the village used to wonder about me having gone for studies but no one knew except my elder brother, about the reason behind being in Delhi. That was a wonder for them but they would tell me to do a job and get married. According to them, the level of my education was more than enough and too much.

During these three years (1977-80), I got many opportunities to attend and participate in several seminars. One such great opportunity was to attend the World Anthropological Congress in New Delhi at Vigyan Bhavan. A few friends and I used to go in a group and attend the sessions that we found interesting and closer to our subjects. There were several reputed anthropologists and sociologists from all over the world. Many of them specialized in Indian anthropology and sociology, especially the North American and British specialists who worked on different issues of the Indian caste system like untouchability, village system, tribes, etc. One such session was on untouchability chaired by Dr. Beatrice Diamond Miller from the US. Her work has been on the ex-untouchables who converted to Buddhism. All of us attended the session with great enthusiasm and interest. I particularly asked the paper presenters a few questions to which Dr. Miller was appreciative and gave me her card. I was in touch with her through letters. She is the one who invited and sponsored my participation in the International Budhhist Studies Conference held at Nalanda in 1980. Also this was a great opportunity in life to visit the Bodh Gaya temple; the place where Lord Buddha attained enlightenment and also meet the Dalai Lama who lived there as a refugee.

English Classes and the Krishnans

Mrs. Shantha Krishnan was on the JNU faculty, wife of Mr. P.S. Krishnan who retired as an IAS officer. A highly respected person and officer in the government machinery, he held several important positions in different offices and devoted his entire career to the cause of the downtrodden communities. Similarly, Mrs. Krishnan has been very kind and sympathetic to all the deprived sections and particularly to the SCs. I met her at her Department of Adult Education in JNU over an academic issue. She was very receptive and respectful to me. She enquired about me and my background and also the problems of SC students in JNU. Being aware of the problems, she organized English language classes for the SC students under a government scheme. These students were research scholars and MA level students. The need was felt due to their poor English language skills that affected their academic performance in addition to adjustment problems with other students and teachers. I tried and coordinated to organize and mobilize the students. The teachers appointed for these sessions were very good and sensitive enough to the cause. One senior professor of linguistics, Dr. M.P. Jain was invited from IIT Delhi to conduct the sessions. Dr. Jain was especially invited from the UK to teach English language and communication skills at the IIT. He was a good teacher. However, the response from the students was poor; maybe due to their pre-occupations or perhaps because they did not realize the importance. Some of them were reluctant and shy, thinking that people would get to know their weakness. Finally nearly 30-35 students turned up. The classes started and continued for three weeks. This was repeated again after a two month gap. The sessions proved to be very useful. This reminds me of the biggest flaw in the government offices and among the academicians and students- that there are several schemes and programmes for development of these communities in education, administration and in life in general. However, neither are the stakeholders aware nor are the government officials and the university administration proactive; probably out of social biases that result in under utilization of funds and poor implementation of schemes. Realizing the importance of such programmes, I saw to it that the schemes were implemented successfully at TISS (Tata Institute of Social Sciences) while holding the position of the Liaison Officer of the SC-ST Cell. People like Mr. and Mrs. Krishnan are very few in the country, the ones who make real efforts with full commitment and enthusiasm for the cause of the downtrodden. Being fully aware of their services to the communities and thereby to the nation, I salute all such known and unknown people who have worked hard in big or small ways for the cause of the deprived sections of Indian society. The Krishnan couple is one of them. After their retirement, I used to meet Mr. Krishnan at the meetings organized by the ministries. Recently in November I met them at their residence in Gurgaon after many years.

A year after I joined TISS, in 1985, the World Sociological Conference took place in New Delhi. Many faculty members, including myself from TISS, participated in the conference. The venue was the Asoka Hotel. One of the sessions on sociology of education proved to be very fruitful for me. I met Prof. Walter Allen of the University of California, Los Angeles during the session. He made a presentation on the higher education of Blacks in the USA. I asked him certain questions and made my points about higher education of the SCs in India and the need to make a comparative study. He appreciated my contribution and gave me his visiting card. Since then we have been in touch with each other. He was a pleasant and friendly person with a good academic calibre. He was very curious to know about Indian untouchables and their plight. He has been sensitive about the issues probably because he is Black and has faced discrimination. He is the one who invited and sponsored my participation in the international seminars organized by him in Italy and China with the outcome of published volumes. I have my contributions published in both volumes. Also he paid for my accommodation charges at the Brisbane World Sociological Conference without my knowledge. However, after his retirement we lost touch with each other. I am very grateful to him, for his active support and encouragement. This is very exceptional for Indian academics.

At a personal level, I applied for study leave to collect the remaining data for my thesis. There was a special provision by the UGC (University Grants Commission) to encourage the faculty to complete their theses. I was sanctioned two months leave with full salary. I went to JNU, stayed in the hostel guest room and started data collection in the DDA Munirka area. At the end, the fixed target of respondents was not met; so I extended it to the government colony nearby with the help of my Punjabi SC friend who was studying at IIT and had a few contacts with SC government employees living in the colony. The experiences were enriching, both socially and academically. I learned many new things. Yet there were a few who refused to cooperate due to their suspicious nature and yet a few more refused to accept that they belonged to the SC community. This was October 1984 when the Prime Minister Indira Gandhi was assassinated.

Before leaving for Mumbai, I discussed the entire plan and strategies to work with the data with my supervisor. After reaching TISS, I consulted a few senior colleagues who were reputed experts in research methodology, data analysis, etc. such as Prof. R.D. Naik and Prof. Hebsur. Prof. Aikara was particularly supportive and encouraging in this regard. He provided real moral and academic motivation for me. Silent by nature, he used to talk less, only as much as required and was sympathetic to all the marginalized people. For data coding and entry into SPSS+ package Mr. Salvi helped. I was fortunate to have such helpful advisors at the TISS. I am thankful to them for their help and support. Thus I could manage the basic and important background work for my thesis. By this time I completed one year of the job. Completing the then existing probation period of one year, I was confirmed and became a full-time regular, permanent employee of the TISS. I got thoroughly involved in my thesis. Coding data, data entry, single frequency, cross tabulation and data analysis was possible because of my advisors. After preparing the scheme of chapters, I decided to visit my supervisor and discuss the plans and further activities about the thesis. However, I was also engaged with official work.

By that time, I had shifted to a rented room from Kurla to Vashi, Navi Mumbai. It was very expensive for me to rent a room in a good locality due to the deposit money and the rental amount. I always used contacts to rent a room. All told, I shifted to 5 places as I was not comfortable in any of the localities. In comparison, the JNU Hostel room was much better and bigger. Then there was the problem of local transportation due to the daily commute to office and back, in addition to expenses including food. In those days although the prices were lower, the cost of the rupee was high. My salary was just enough to survive in the expensive Mumbai city. There was no question of asking my brother or father for money. Somehow I used to manage. I found it very difficult to adjust to the Mumbai life and culture. It took a long time for me to settle down. It was a fast life. No one had time to talk, interact or show much concern at a personal level. I found it dry, mechanical and artificial. Roda Billimoria and Padma Velaskar were research scholars at TISS and helpful to me. They were close to me and always empathized with my troubles and supported me. Sometimes I would think of giving up the job and moving back to JNU and join my friends there. But I knew it was too big a risk to give up a permanent job. I always felt lonely; more so after office hours. I had no friends, no close relatives, no one to talk to and share my feelings and difficulties.

The Second Job: After successful completion of the MPhil degree, I was looking for a job. My supervisor advised and recommended me for a job at the Indian Institute of Education (IIE), Pune. There were two main purposes behind it; one was that I would improve research skills and gain experience besides some income. The job was as research assistant for a project on SC identity. I was to work under Prof. A.B. Shah, the director of the project. So I shifted to Pune and stayed in the Institute guest house. I enjoyed the work and it was a great thing for me to work with Prof. Shah who was very well known for his academic and intellectual level. A rationalist and secularist in principle and practice, he was highly regarded in the city, state and the country. He was very sympathetic to all the downtrodden, particularly the SCs. In spite of being a Gujarati Jain, he used to have all kinds of non-vegetarian food. He was a very strict but kind person. He often helped me going out of his way. I learned many things from him.

The office was located in a rented private bungalow close to the Film Institute of India. Most of the staff and faculty were older/retired from their jobs. Only three of us were young—a steno, junior librarian and myself. We used to be together most of the time over tea and lunch. The steno was a Christian lady from Kerala, the librarian was a hardcore Brahmin and myself an SC. No one knew my caste except Prof. Shah.

The entire environment in the office was Brahminical with typical Brahminical attitude of a superiority complex. The difference between feudal and dominant culture and the mass culture was very clear and open. Firstly between their looks and skin colour difference (fair skin) and secondly in the language that they spoke as against the language common people speak. They used to generally make fun of my Marathi and kept correcting me. I used to laugh at their Hindi and English. The Marathi librarian lady being Brahmin would correct my Marathi and I her Hindi/English. Unknowingly she and I got closer as friends because she was a trained classical Hindustani singer with a melodious and sweet voice and I was a trained classical dancer. Both of us had a sense of music. One day on the terrace of the building I persuaded her to sing a song. She sang in Lata Mangeshkar's voice that I liked and appreciated. By then we were very close to each other and used to go out in the city after office hours and have fun. We were finally attracted to each other. At the end we, the librarian and I, decided to marry. One day we decided to meet in a park to take the final decision about marriage. She came with her uncle. We started discussing and suddenly he asked me about my caste to which I replied openly. Immediately he told me marriage was not possible because of my caste. She kept quiet, perhaps agreeing with her uncle. I was surprised to see her silence. I had anticipated this and was mentally prepared to face it. I also quickly assented to the decision without any hesitation. We said goodbye to each other and departed forever. After a few days she left the job and joined another office. I was already thinking of giving up the job and going back to JNU. It was the last month of my job after serving for nine months. I conveyed my decision of leaving to Prof. Shah. The project data collection was completed and only two more months were left to complete my tenure. Prof. Shah agreed and permitted me to leave the job and go back to JNU. During my 10-month stay in Pune I did not enjoy myself much; however, I did make some friends at the National Defence Academy (NDA) and the Film & Television Institute of India (FTII).

Finally in June 1980, I left for Delhi with a limited amount of money. I could not save at all in Pune because the salary was fixed and just enough to maintain myself. Repenting my decision to have gone to Pune for such a job, I got registered at JNU for my PhD and got the same room in the same Sutlej Hostel where I had stayed from day one. I had to borrow money from friends till I renewed my UGC fellowship. Thus the JNU days began again. This time I had developed a lot of confidence and self-respect. Prof. Karuna Chanana used to listen carefully, try to understand problems and academic issues. She was a good teacher as she allowed questions, encouraged participation in class and general interaction. She was known for being a strict and disciplined teacher but good at heart and open to knowing things. Yet I always felt social distance with her and a complex of gender difference; maybe, it was due to my socialization in the male dominated family. I continued to feel the same for many more years.

Marriage and Family

My parents and my brother were by now pressurizing me for marriage. However they wanted me to choose for myself (a change in values and custom). I placed an advertisement in the matrimonial section of the *Times of India* with my caste, education and occupational details with no caste bar. Surprisingly, I got responses only from the SC/Buddhist communities. One such lady directly came to me in the office alone, with no prior notice, to propose to me. I did not know how to handle the situation. But somehow I managed to say no to her. She insisted that I visit her house in a suburb of Mumbai city. I went to her house with a friend. After seeing the home environment, I decided firmly not to accept the proposal. The same lady again came to my office after a month with her two male relatives to propose. But by that time, my marriage was already fixed at Dhule through a distant relative of hers who got introduced to me through someone. The caste ties are stronger when it comes to marriage and social discourse; although I was consciously willing to marry out of caste, preferably a girl from the Matang caste. That is, inter-caste among the SCs because the trend among the inter caste marriages showed that most of such marriages have been between SC boys and Brahmin girls; at least in Maharashtra as far I know. Besides this, it is observed that no other upper castes, including Brahmins, accept the girls from SCs due to the stereotype or the belief that it will pollute their progeny and the *Vansh* as the women are treated as low and inferior to men in the patriarchal society. The Matang community is estimated to be the second highest in the state with 32 per cent, as against 35 per cent Mahar community out of the total SC population in the state. This community has been treated as the lowest in the social hierarchy traditionally, and historically deprived—socially, culturally and in current times politically. This could be because the Matangs did/do not have strong leadership and have been under the influence of the Congress Party. There have been deliberate attempts to keep the Matangs, Chambhars, Dhors and others (with a few exceptions) away from Dr. Ambedkar's movement to the extent that Dr. Ambedkar had to face strong opposition from these castes on all fronts including political, to the extent that Dr. Ambedkar was defeated in the election by a SC

Chambhar rival who was a Congress Party candidate. It may be noted that there are 1,092 SC castes in the country and 59 officially recognized castes in Maharashtra. Out of which there are 5 major castes in Maharashtra: namely, Mahar, Matang (called Mang in daily usage), Chambhar, Dhor and Holer. These castes have also been victims of untouchability and ban on inter-dining.The hierarchy is such—Chambhars are socially on top followed by Dhors and then Mahars and at the bottom the Matangs. Other castes are treated as minor demographically, due to their insignificant number. So these communities got deprived of the social reform movement programme launched by Dr. Ambedkar including religious conversion, in addition to his call to give up traditional occupations. The Chambhars still continue their leather-based occupation and it has a demand in the market even today and in the case of Matangs, they continue their traditional occupation like drum beating and broom making that gives them very poor income. They still continue to follow the *balutedari* and *vatan* system in many villages of the state. Lack of education, unawareness, poverty, etc. forced them to depend on upper castes more than other castes even today. I have seen many families in some parts of the state continue to eat dead animals even today. Thus the politics of the Congress Party was successful, to a great extent, in using these castes against Dr. Ambedkar socially and politically, and portraying him as the leader of only the Mahars.

Therefore, I could attribute my failure in getting a life partner from other communities among the SCs and particularly from the Matang community for these reasons. I was not actually willing to get married because there was a call from the conscience to work for these communities on a full-time basis. However, I was compelled by the circumstances to change my decision.

I was always worried about my thesis and its completion and worked hard for it. The head of the Unit was liberal enough to give me more space to complete my PhD. After completing the background work, I went to Delhi to discuss with my guide who was very cooperative. I made two-three such trips; each time giving one or two chapters for corrections. At the same time, at TISS I was assigned to work for the Indian Sociological Society as business manager on an honorary basis. Prof. Chitnis was elected secretary of the society and its office was based in the Unit. This took two years of my time just working for the society attending to everything; correspondence, maintaining records and the accounts, and dispatching the bulletin to all the members. I was not happy with this work but had no other option. The only incentive given was to attend the Indian Sociological Conference at Shillong with air travel provision.

However, the thesis work got further delayed due to my marriage, starting from proposal formalities to marriage and post marriage formalities. It was an arranged marriage. Vijaya's distant relative brought the proposal from Dhule. He took me to Dhule to see the girl. I was accompanied by a friend of mine. After reaching the place, this relative went to his nearby native village on some pretext and never came back. This gentleman smartly made me spend money for everything. I am sure he had some urgent work in his village and that is why he made me go with him in a short time. While leaving the place, I told the people I would go ahead with marriage only after my parents and elder brother approved of the proposal. After a few days my father and elder brother came to see the girl and I joined them. This time everything was discussed including marriage expenses. Of course no one from either side demanded dowry. But small gifts of gold jewellery was expected and they agreed. It was also decided that all the expenses would be shared equally. The wedding date fixed was November 27, 1985 and the venue of the wedding was Akola, a district town about 60 kilometres away from my village. It was mutually decided to have a simple and inexpensive ceremony. Once again all our relatives gathered in Dhule for marriage shopping and the ring ceremony was completed. Finally, the wedding day dawned. It was a simple wedding with Buddhist rituals exactly on time at 11 am in the morning. Then all of us went to the village along with the bride. Despite several requests, no one from the bride's side came to my village. They all went back to Dhule. She was all alone which was against the custom. In the village the *Barat* was taken out in the late evening. Then all of us returned to Parbhani where my elder brother was working. After that both Vijaya and I went to Dhule to meet her relatives. As a custom, after marriage the bride is supposed to be brought back to her *Maher* (parental place) by a close relative. In this case neither was there anyone to accompany her nor anyone to take her back. Therefore my family members suggested that I take her back myself. Vijaya was surprised to see my people and their customs and language which is a mixture of Marathi and Urdu with a typical Varhadi accent. Similarly, I was surprised at their Ahirani language which is a mixture of Marathi, Gujarati and Urdu. Both these dialects are different from the established Marathi which is Brahminical and used in education all over Maharashtra. It seemed they were not happy with us due to their internal family disputes. I was shocked and surprised to see the quarrels among themselves. We, the newly married couple were not welcomed. The reasons behind this are not really known to me. After an overnight stay, we came back to Mumbai.

I rented a small room with a kitchenette after paying a deposit in Vashi, Navi Mumbai. After a few months my nephew joined us for his studies. He left Mumbai after a year as he was not able to adjust with us and his school was far away in Chembur. During this year my mother joined us for a month or so. She also went back home as she too found it difficult to adjust. Her frequent complaints used to be about keeping the door closed during the day time. In villages people hardly ever keep it closed.

Vijaya was renamed as Radha by now. Genarally the custom of renaming the newly wed in Maharashtra is common among all the castes. By now Radha was pregnant and expecting a baby. After the seventh month rituals she was taken for delivery at her *Maher* with her consent. This is another custom to deliver the first baby at the parental home.

I had tentatively decided not to marry in life and devote time for social causes; and if at all I married it would be to a woman from the Matang community. But both promises proved to be self-broken due to my casual approach to marriage.

In October, we were blessed with a baby girl Shweta. After a gap of two years a baby boy was born at Radha's parental home called Vikrant. By now we shifted to the TISS campus residence that was long awaited. This was a big house with all the facilities available and just a five-minute walk from my office room.

Now we were a family of four. Radha got a teacher's job at a high school in Matunga. It used to very difficult for her to travel early in the moring for the job and also look after children carefully and maintain the house. Her health was severely affected. After serious thought, we decided that Radha should give up the job to take better care of the children who were growing happily. However, it was a diffcult to get on financially. Somehow we used to manage. The children then were going to school beginning with KG classes and continued till the 10th standard in the same schools. The schools were known as the best convent schools in Chembur run by Christian priests; separate for boys and girls in the same premises behind the Catholic Church. This reminds of me of my schools and Radha's schools where we studied and the struggle we under went. After completing the 10th, we never forced Shweta or Vikrant to opt for any particular course when there was a craze for technical/professional education. However, Shweta was keen on going for a medical degree. She joined Vivekanand College with the Arts sream as she could not get into the Science stream even under the reserved quota due to cut throat competition. Here Shweta experienced open caste based discrimation in our presence, by a college teacher who was handling the admissions. Vikrant joined Ram Narayan Ruia College with the Arts stream. Both these colleges are run by the RSS lobby. Further, both of them completed their Masters in Sociology (all 4 of us are MA with Sociology). Shweta did her MA from JNU after her law degree and Vikrant from the Delhi School of Economics. Currently both are working in Delhi. Both Radha and I are happy about their achievements and feel proud of their English language and communication skills (I recall my weakness here). Both help me correcting English language and academic writings. They are now adult and they fully enjoy their freedom of everything including awaited marriage. I call it a matter of educational environment, training and opportunities available for one. It has certainly created a generation gap between parents and children with upward and relatively smooth mobility. I began with zero, they began with all the facilities available. At last, just to confess, the relationship between Radha and myself has been somewhat uncomfortable due to a communication gap or different upbringing. Both of us are happy and live in Navi Mumbai with a pet dog Neo.

My Love for the Arts

I must admit that my real inclination has been towards music and dance. This could be attributed to my father who used to perform for the *gammat*. Till date, it has been my constant companion; despite all the odds and contradictions in life. I continue to act, react and respond to any musical rhythm. During childhood, I used to sing and dance on my own behind closed doors of the house whenever no one was at home; may be out of shame or fear. Now I realize that it was because I would be ridiculed for dancing in spite of being a boy. This slowly led to a tendency to avoid expressing myself musically and to supress my inclination to dance. In the absence of a nurturing environment and guidance, one could describe it as an act of killing an art and the urge to express oneself artistically.

It was only at college level I realized that this is an art gifted by nature and there is nothing wrong in doing it. I then started participating in the college annuals—acting in plays, dancing in a group and solo and also as a female with costumes. Unfortunately, all those acts of mine invited teasing and ridicule by many college fellows. As a result, I used to feel hurt and humiliated. This led to avoiding such activities to keep myself away from such humiliation and insults. This is a typical example of the average Indian mindset made out of a strong caste and gender bias that deprives one of the basic freedom to express and enjoy oneself. Attributing things to good and bad, to pure and impure, and male and female to acts and expressions, are a part of the basic cultural and social complex in our society.

It was only after joining JNU as a research scholar,

that I could rethink and reorganize myself to start learning and performing dance and music freely. This was more due to the free and open social and academic environment in the university campus. I started participating in various programmes like hostel night, Holi celebration, annual function, etc. Generally students and teachers used to appreciate me and my art. Finally, I decided to join a formal classical dance class and joined Triveni Kala Sangam at Mandi House to learn Bharatnatyam. The fee was reasonable but the distance and the transportation used to be a problem. There I started learning the dance under the teachings of Guru Krishna Kumar. He used to find it difficult to pronounce my surname (as I was known), he gave me a new name 'Arvind'. Here after I started using the new name whenever I used to perform or learn and also tell close friends to call me by the new name. Eventually, the learning of Bharatnatyam at Triveni went on for a year or more. There used to be an elderly French woman with me, who had come all the way from Paris. There were four-five other girls in my class and no other male student. Somehow I used to feel that I was not enjoying the dance form and at times hesitated to learn steps and expressions along with females.

Finally, I decided to discontinue Bharatnatyam and learn Kathak where you find more male dancers as compared to Bharatnatyam. It is also due to the footwork and expressions it teaches besides freedom of movement. However, due to the distance between the JNU campus and the dance centre, the cost of the commute was high as there was no direct bus. All the well known dance and music schools were funded by the government and located in the Mandi House area within a close vicinity. I joined one called Bharatiya Kala Kendra and started learning Kathak there. After a few months I realized that time was a problem, although classes used to be twice a week. This was in addition to my regular research classes. Of course my priority was regular studies. Subsequently, I decided to discontinue and invite a junior teacher to the hostel to teach me. Luckily, I got one from the Kathak Kendra charging a reasonable fee who used to stay close to the JNU campus. With the permission of the hostel warden I started learning under the new guru. This went on till I gave my first Kathak performance at the students' night under the guidance of the teacher. I was so happy, excited and enjoying myself thoroughly. But somehow here too I found some detractors making fun of me saying that I was practising a "female" dance form. By now I had become bold and learned not to care for such negative remarks. This went on for some time till I left JNU and joined work at TISS, Mumbai. After joining TISS as lecturer, I again started looking for a dance class which was found near TISS in a private house. The teacher used to come here from Goregaon once in a while but the disciple of the main guru used to conduct the class. The disciple was a woman. Finally, we shifted the class to the TISS campus. There was one more girl and a boy learning with me. This also went on for some time. Here I took a prolonged gap due to my marriage and the long trip to Germany. After returning, the other dancer and I gave a performance at the TISS annual function. Radha and the children saw my dance and greatly appreciated it. They have always been appreciative of my dance. Often Radha or Vikrant or Shweta asked me to do some poses at home and I complied to their requests. My dedication was such that I bought a harmonium, *tabla* and *ghunghroos*. I wished greatly that at least one of our children becomes an artist. They did begin with learning *tabla* and *Hindustani* vocal but gave up after some time having developed a liking for Western music; it could be due to the schools they went to that were run by Christian missionaries with emphasis on Western culture.

At last I was compelled to fully stop dance due to a major jerk received in the waist while performing on the TISS annual day. This was a bad ending to my passion and love of dance. I remember, my research supervisor Prof. Karuna Chanana suggested that I make a career in dance; however, I missed it for several reasons and more so due to lack of confidence caused by social and cultural ideas associated with masculinity and dance. I think it is an odd mixture of appreciation and derision that is reserved for a male dancer. The classical forms of the arts have been traditionally the domain of the upper caste elite (more so the Brahmins) unlike folk arts. However, dance and music continues to be a part of me. I still continue to listen and watch on television classical and semi-classical music, songs and dances from old Hindi films of the 1960s, 1970s and 1980s. Lata Mangeshkar, Mohammad Rafi and Asha Bhosle are my favourite singers, while the acclaimed Gopi Krishna and Birju Maharj are my ideals for Kathak. Lastly, please allow me to mention, I keep expressing dance gestures and give poses over songs and music at home even now. I am a dab hand at choreography too!.

Back to JNU: The PhD

I had several discussions with the supervisor on the doctoral topic. I wanted to continue with the same topic of education and occupational mobility and the SCs but with larger scope and depth. Finally the topic was decided mutually. I started doing a review of literature in the area and then got into writing the proposal. After several drafts, the proposal was approved and I gave a proposal presentation. The task was difficult for me mainly due to the academic language. Taking notes, referencing, taking points, quoting authors, building up arguments, articulation, etc have been skills I have acquired and are very interesting steps in research at this stage. This experience was relaxing after going through the MPhil stage. As an insider, I used to say more, argue more and add more to the issues of the SCs. Prof. Chanana used to listen, encourage and appreciate this. I always believed (and still believe) that the education system along with the social system has been equally responsible for deprivation in society. The education is clearly dividing the students and teachers across caste, class and gender line and more so on the rural-urban divide besides the language, i.e. vernacular versus English. Those who succeed in accessing education suffer from various kinds of social, psychological and academic problems. This hampers their performance and academic creativity directly which ultimately results in moral and academic discouragement and feeling of being suffocated in all ways. In fact, all those coming from rural, poor and socially deprived backgrounds, actually possess rich and direct actual experiences and observations that would enrich the academic and research discourse in our country. However, the system makes you forget/ suppress such richness of lived experiences and reduce it to a minimum and superficial academic out product. The entire world of social sciences has been like this; more so the sociology and education fields. I say this because I have been the student and learner of these disciplines for several decades. Most of the works in these areas tend to be superficial; be it a caste or untouchabilty issue or educational issues.

After successful proposal presentation, I prepared the interview schedule for data collection, The universe of the study was the educated and employed SCs residing in DDA (Delhi Development Authority) Munirka locality, New Delhi that is just close to the JNU campus. The rationale was that there were very few studies in this area of research. The DDA office being the government body, followed the reservations for SC-ST in allotment of the housing scheme, and the employees were working at the high and middle level positions in government departments. I happened to know a few of the SC residents in the colony which made it easy for me to enter their world. As to what background they came from, what was their educational and occupational background and what were their experiences on caste lines in the neighbourhood which was a mixed type, were some basic points of enquiry in my research.

Money was not a problem in those days as I was getting the UGC fellowship or else it would have thoroughly impacted my motivation and the work. After pre-testing the interview schedule, I procured the list of SC residents and prepared the list of potential respondents with their names and addresses. Before I started the fieldwork, I made some visits and met a few of them again to build a rapport. Surprisingly, most of them were socially aware and very cooperative. But they used to take time to open up. Most of them used to be curious first to know about my caste and then only would feel comfortable and freely answer the questions. The reason behind asking about my caste they gave was that they did not trust the non-SC researchers because they do not write properly and correctly about problems of the SCs being biased socially. Thus it took more than a year to start with the data collection. During the fieldwork, the experiences have been of many types: good and bad, frustrating and encouraging. Many used to welcome me and my topic, some used to discourage me saying that such research was meaningless and nothing would happen except earning me a PhD degree. Yet some other people would suspect my integrity and intentions.

Some with hidden caste identity would refuse to talk to me and deny that they belong to SC. A few living with hidden caste identity and pretending to be upper caste asked me to get out of the house and not to talk about caste and SC matters. Such were these highly educated officers caught between their real and false identities: caste with stigma on one hand and secular modern existence with education and modern secular occupations. Most of them were first generation educated SCs full of struggle coming from different states of India. The ones who were followers of Dr. Ambedkar were seen to be more open, confident and proud of their mission and struggle. The data collection was extended to the neighbouring government staff colony called RK Puram as the required number of respondents was not complete. This was done by using the snow ball method. One of the days was October 31, 1984, the day of horror, violence and fear all around. The then Prime Minister Indira Gandhi was assassinated. I was on fieldwork collecting data. After I came out of a house, I was told about the incident. All around the colony and other localities the Sikhs were targeted, attacked and killed. Their houses were burnt. The individual Sikhs were singled out from buses and vehicles and beaten up. I saw this with my own eyes before rushing to JNU. The riots went on for four-five days. One fine morning a Sikh was passing through JNU campus hiding from the rioting crowd. He walked through the jungles the whole night. We students showed him right way to move away from the spots where the riots were taking place. Thus we tried to save his life. A few of the Sikh students in the hostels were given special protection by the students. Throughout the four-five riot days, the supply of milk, vegetables, and groceries were not available in the hostels. We used to have black tea and simple *rotis* with *daal* and managed somehow to carry on. Everything was disturbed in the city. The public transport, offices and markets were shut down. Those were the horrifying days that I can never forget in my life. I could not believe such a tragic death of a leader like Indira Gandhi; the prime minister of such a big democratic country. My fieldwork was held up for a few days till the situation became normal. After that, I resumed the fieldwork again. It took another two months to complete it.

While the fieldwork was on, I saw an advertisement of the Tata Institute of Social Sciences (TISS) in the classified column of the *Times of India* daily for recruitment of the faculty positions.There were 16 lecturer positions reserved for SC-ST at the TISS. I applied for the lecturer position at the Unit for Research in Sociology of Education (URSE) on the advice of Prof. Chanana.

As I had a firm desire to try for the civil services also conducted by the UPSC (Union Public Services); after completing the MPhil course, I joined Rao's IAS (Indian Administrative Services) Coaching Centre. In any case, while leaving for Delhi I had decided to take two challenges; one was clearing the IAS exam and second to acquire the PhD degree. After joining JNU, I got more inspired for the IAS because of the entirely encouraging and inspirational environment due to students' orientation and their efforts to prepare for this competitive examination. Many students would every year take this exam. The library facilities and the open discussions among students and their willingness to work hard would encourage one to aspire for the IAS. The students were really talented and intelligent and very supportive of each other. To my great surprise, two-three students used to write study material for the UPSC exam and students would buy that from them. In turn, every year, around 10-20 students used to pass and join various services including the IFS, IAS, IPS and Allied services.

Taking this exam while doing the course was not officially allowed but the teachers and the administration would knowingly ignore it. As long as their UPSC preparations were never at the cost of regular studies, they used to manage both very carefully and systematically. A few only used to join coaching centres. I joined it mainly because the Home Ministry paid my coaching fees under a special scheme for the SC-ST development. This scheme still continues for the SC-ST for other exams such as the medical and engineering entrance and to study abroad, besides training for jobs and remedial coaching like English language, communication skills and personality development. But unfortunately all these schemes and programmes in operation are being poorly implemented because of the bureaucracy, biases and the hard eligibility criteria. Most importantly, it is the lack of awareness among the stakeholders that is the culprit. In those days the government used to advertise such schemes in English daily newspapers. The scheme to study abroad is known as National Overseas Scholarship scheme that was introduced by the Government of India in 1954 with the concerted efforts of Dr. Ambedkar. Till recently the number of such scholarships was 54, now reduced to 34 as I understand.

The fees at the Rao Study Circle was heavy and of course I could not afford them otherwise. There were a few more SC-ST students with me from JNU and outside under the scheme. The centre was located on Hailey Road. There was no direct bus available those days to travel from JNU to Hailey Road. One had to walk a distance at both the ends. The classes were from the morning 7.30 am till 1 pm. So we had to leave JNU without breakfast in the morning and buy and eat lunch at the centre in the afternoon. All this in the chilly cold of the morning. The coaching went on for six months after which I appeared for the preliminary and cleared it. Just before the main exam, however, I fell ill and could not make it.

JNU has always been a matter of attraction, curiosity and surprise for local Delhites, especially the youth. They all used to greatly admire the academic standards and the talent of the teachers and students. But surprisingly, there used to be a very negligible number of students from Delhi city itself studying at JNU. Their perceptions were that the JNU community is free and open for everything including girls and hence many of them used to make friends with JNU students and visit the campus to have fun. There were a few SC students from IIT also visiting me. One such person came into contact with me. He lived close by in the old locality (Jia Sarai). He was a Brahmin originally from Delhi and studying for the degree course in a college. He did not know my caste at this stage. Also he introduced me to his friend who was also studying in a college and living in the same locality. He was a Sindhi. His parents were refugees from Karachi who migrated at the time of partition. The Brahmin was decent and mature and later I used to borrow money from him in the case of need and urgency. He used to write for Hindi magazines. The Sindhi was immature, vocal and cranky. His father was working for DTC (Delhi Transport Services) office as a time keeper. The Brahmin and I visited each other's residences. His parents were very helpful and kind. His father was a school teacher. Whenever I felt home sick I would visit them. His mother used to give me tea and sometimes food to eat. We were very close friends, so one day I revealed my caste to him. He was surprised and did not believe me initially. But he told this to the Sindhi guy. Then he started taunting me about caste, reservation policy and talked non-stop about how the SCs were getting benefits they did not deserve. At the end, we used to get into heated arguments and confrontations. I slowly made out clearly that both families were ignorant of the issue and biased against the community. However none of them showed any difference in their behaviour towards me, at least in my presence. After two-three years both of them got a government job. The Brahmin got married. I attended the wedding. Later I noticed that his wife was a typical orthodox Brahmin who hailed from a suburb with in the vicinity of Delhi city and was a Sanskrit teacher. They did not have any issue for five-seven years. They went for medical treatment in Delhi initially and after a year or so the couple came to Mumbai for treatment. By the time I was at TISS staying on the campus with my wife Radha and my baby Shweta. I invited them home. They came and very firmly refused to have anything; not even water on the pretext of having had everything already. I knew this but Radha was surprised and felt bad and told me not to entertain them anymore. Both of us felt very bad. And that was the beginning of weakening the friendship. We have no more relations and contacts with the couple.

6

What Do Testing Times Prove to Us?

It was November 1983, while the data collection was in full swing. I received an interview call from TISS for the lecturer's position. I left for Mumbai to attend the personal interview, leaving the data collection work in between. It was discovered that in all there were 16 positions vacant under the reserved quota meant for SC-ST in different departments. This was a backlog to be filled. God knows who and why took the decision to fill these positions. I suppose it was Prof. Suma Chitins who pursued and convinced the Governing Board and the Director Prof. Armaity Desai about the policy and its need to implement it. May be because she was one of the senior most faculty and head of the URSE (Unit for Research in Sociology of Education) and her entire work was on education of the SCs. Prof. Chanana and Prof. Chitnis knew each other professionally. Prof. Chitnis was my external examiner for the MPhil dissertation.

Out of all the candidates who appeared for personal interview, only two were recruited—one for ST and one for SC (myself). And all the remaining posts were deserved and thrown open for general candidates and recruited subsequently. Later it was discovered that the great TISS implemented the reservation policy only in 1981. Certainly it was unsocial and unlawful on the part of TISS, which was known for social work with an academic reputation.

Luckily I was given accommodation in the hostel for three days and was reimbursed the travel fare. I knew no one in Mumbai. The interview was satisfactory.

I went back to Delhi and restarted the fieldwork for my doctoral dissertation. In March I got a letter from TISS that I was selected for the position. I was very happy but worried about the data collection and completion of my thesis. I met Prof. Chanana and told her I would join the job only after I completed the data collection. She advised and insisted that I should join at the earliest. I accepted the offer and informed TISS that I would join after a month. This was March 1984. I had to wind up everything. Application to deregister from the JNU roll, vacate the hostel, arrange to pack up books and other belongings and so on. I informed the UGC about the job with thanks for the fellowship and to discontinue the fellowship. I packed the books and kept them at the house of a fellow in RK Puram who was in a government job but was an RSS (Rashtriya Swyamsevak Sangh) worker through a sympathizer of an RSS friend from JNU. The same friend helped me get a letter from the RSS head office in Delhi for my stay at the RSS head office in Mumbai. I stayed in the Mumbai RSS head office for a week because I had no other option as I had no friends and relatives known to me in Mumbai. Besides, staying out in a lodge or hotel was not affordable for me. However, while taking back the books, the JNU friend kept many of my good books for himself that he never returned. I felt bad but could not say no to him. All my friends in JNU were happy about my job. They wished me luck. One fine morning I boarded the train for Bombay (then), now Mumbai along with a Maharashtrian friend who was studying with me. He had relatives in Mumbai and had some work there on his way to his village. We reached Mumbai and went straight to the RSS head office. It was an office with a few rooms to stay for visitors. The friend was reluctant and unhappy (so was I) with my decision to go and stay at the RSS office because both of us were against the RSS ideology that preaches and practices Brahminical ideology and considered to be against all the downtrodden. But I was helpless and somehow prepared my mind to take a chance. After submitting the letter that I got from the Delhi RSS office, the person in charge gave us a simple room without asking any questions except for our original place and the purpose for visiting Mumbai. In the evening we wandered around the places. Next day the friend and I went to the TISS just to get familiar with the route and the public transportation. In the evening he left for his relative's place. I was alone, feeling strange, many people visiting and staying in the office. There was one disabled fellow from Kerala who was on a world tour on a bicycle and was being sponsored by the RSS organization. Two days later, I decided to join the office. In the meanwhile, I had already informed my elder brother about my job selection and about the accommodation problem. He had his distant relative through his wife living in Chembur closer to the TISS campus. Two days later the relative (Bhabhi's Mama), an elderly person, came to TISS to meet me. A very kind and talkative person conversing in English, he asked me to stay with him. I used to call him Uncle. His was a big family, all living in one small house in Subhash Nagar. After two days, his elder son came with me to the RSS office to pick up my bags. We came back to Subhash Nagar. Thus I shifted to uncle's place. Everyone welcomed me. There were six members living in such a small house. I was the seventh one. It was my first time to meet them. I felt shy, reluctant and uncomfortable. The man's wife was cranky, but they took care of me and gave me food and support very promptly and regularly. They used to feel happy and proud of me, my education and the job and tell the neighbours and other people about me. Thus I stayed with them for a month or so. Finally his elder son helped me get a room to stay in Kurla through his social contacts.

The Travails of Work

It was on April 10, 1984, that I joined the first permanent job at the TISS, a supposedly reputed institute with academic excellence. At times I used to be incredulous that someone with such humble beginnings like me had actually joined such an institution. The Unit for Research in Sociology of Education (URSE) was headed by Prof. J. Aikara in the absence of Prof. Suma Chitnis who was on long leave. There were two more faculty members; Mr. J. Heriques and Dr. K.S. Mondal. One more member was Dr. Denzil Saldanha, who joined two months after I joined the Unit. It was a small research Unit and the faculty of the Unit also used to teach courses to Social Work students. After completing the formalities, I submitted the joining report. Prof. Aikara took me around the units and departments and introduced me to the other faculty members. It was possible to meet everyone personally because those days the institute was small with just 100 students for postgraduate degree (both juniors and seniors) and ten-twelve students for PhD. The main degrees offered were Social Work and Personnel Management. As a junior, I was offered a shared room as my office. After two months a room was vacant so I shifted there. By that time Dr. Saldanha joined. He had a long working experience. He was asked to share the office room with me. He occupied the main sitting place with table and chairs and I was given a side space with one table and one chair. I was given a short briefing about the Institute, the Unit activities and the research work. After two-three months, Prof. Suma Chitnis resumed her work. As a lecturer, this was another totally new experience in my life, bringing its own mixed feelings of anxiety and curiosity, along with feelings of achievement and satisfaction. Never had I imagined, that I would get such a job after attaining high educational qualifications. At times I used to get excited recalling childhood, school days, college days and the university days and the problems faced and overcoming them against all odds. I wrote to my father, uncle and aunt and all other close relatives about my job. Sadly, no one knew how prestigious it was except my elder brother. They only knew I had moved to Mumbai for a job. They were only concerned about the regular income part of it. They were all happy and mother thanked God for giving me a job and rescuing me from all hardships, bad conditions and poverty. This was certainly upward mobility in terms of education and occupation as well as the entry into a new world of academics, intellect and an elite class with Western sophistication. This was denouncing the traditional imposed life of helplessness, poverty, disrespect and dependence. This was freedom from the burden of caste, untouchabilty, humiliation, indignity and hunger. I always ask myself; who should be held responsible for such a degraded human life. Is it religion, caste, society or Indian culture? Or is it the upper castes, Brahmins who propounded and practised such inhuman traditions and made millions of people suffer in society for centuries together? Ultimately I would call it a complete social disorder of the Indian culture with several symptoms of ill health.

It is the great saviour and surgeon who was born after many centuries in this land who rescued millions from this hell and conducted the mission to kill all the social and cultural evils. I speak of none other than the illustrious Babasaheb Bhimrao Amedkar! I bow my head and salute him for his services and contributions in all the fields of the Indian nation and society, particularly his work for the former untouchable communities. Suppose he was not born or had not taken up the cause of these people, I truly wonder where my people and I would have been today. I refer to Babasaheb as my second father who gave me a new birth, dignity and respect. The rest stand far away from the curtain. I fully realized what he said about education as a great means of change, liberty and dignity. His message, "Educate, Unite and Agitate" has been the triumph of social revolution in India. We hardly find a leader of his calibre and stature anywhere in the world; at the same time, we do not find such a suppressive, complex, diverse and hierarchical society with such inhuman practices like compelling humans to eat dead animals and to carry human excreta on their heads. At times I get confused whether I should be proud or ashamed of my country and its culture. Anyway, to enter into a new white collar job and work with the established upper caste educated elites who still continue to carry their prejudices and impose and dominate in academics (with rare exceptions), were and still are major for first generation learners and academicians.

I was invited by a colleague to join the sponsored research project on education of SCs and STs in Maharashtra. It involved data collection from sampled districts. My involvement had the additional benefit of language in the field. It was a new challenge for me. I was deeply involved in data collection with the research staff. I was exposed to new things and facts about rural life, caste, untouchability, education, exploitation, etc. in different parts of the state. It added to my knowledge and sensitivity and I thought I was much better than many others. My colleague and I completed the project jointly and submitted to the funding agency. It was a very gainful experience doing research out of the routine academic framework. After that I was asked by the senior to go to IIT (Indian Institute of Technology), Delhi to collect data for the book/project. I went and got some useful data. My actual experiences at this point were so negative, hurting and humiliating to the extent that I had to wait outside to meet them like a student. Finally I expressed my grievances to the Director. There are many people who have the tendency to cultivate sycophancy and force complete subservience from their colleagues. Sadly such is the psychology of the upper caste elites including academics in general. At the same time they like to display favouritism towards some colleagues and students, while ironically teaching equality and justice in the class. Thus, I had no real moral support at this point. I used to feel frustrated and was at the end of my tether. I had not started teaching yet. After six months or so, the colleague who joined after me and shared the room was promoted as Reader. After he became Reader, he asked me to find another place to sit and he wanted to sit alone as Reader. The practice was that only Professors and Readers were entitled to a single room. Then I was given a place to sit with stenos and clerks. I had no option but to sit with them. It used to be very disturbing because of incoming and outgoing persons in the steno room and above all the typewriting sounds. I pleaded and requested for some other place. Then I was given a place to sit in a classroom and thereafter in a small erected room with wooden sheets under the staircase. After that I was moved to a room on the second floor while the Unit was on the ground floor. Thus, I did not get a room to sit in the office for ten years. Yet another person who joined as lecturer five years after I joined occupied the vacant room in my absence. Whether this can be considered it as discrimination or deprivation, I leave to the readers. There was also an element of favouritism in appointment and promotion in the Unit. I had to wait for ten years to reach the Reader level. At the same time, I must acknowledge the support and encouragement I was given by some other colleagues such as Dr. Padma Velaskar and Dr. Denzil Saldanha in the Unit. This support was both material and non-material, first when Dr. Velaskar as a PhD scholar and then as my colleague. Her support helped considerably to sustain me academically, materially and emotionally. She was very close to Prof. Chitnis as her student. The environment at TISS was certainly elitist with a Western influence in those days. A majority of the students and faculty belonged to an urban, middle class background and were English educated. People hardly spoke in local languages other than English even out of academics. I used to get surprised, especially considering that a course like Social Work needs to have knowledge and exposure to the local culture and language. How these people managed the field work practices, was a question that baffled me. Many Social Work students used to complain about their discomfort in the field, especially over the unhygienic conditions in slums. Some used to argue over poverty and caste as non-existence issues in the days. There used to be very few students from rural, economically challenged, vernacular and SC-ST backgrounds. The faculty colleagues used to complain and show informally their discomfort about these students due to their poor language skills and learning abilities. They found it difficult to guess my caste. There are many surnames in Maharashtra and all India level that clearly indicate one's caste, hence superiority—social, cultural and intellectual, such as Deshpandey, Kulkarni, Joshi, Phadnis, Mishra, Tripathi, Tiwari, Thakur, Yadav and so on. My last name is common among all the castes except for Brahmins in Maharashtra culture. Assuming that I belonged to some upper caste, the same colleagues and students used to be critical of the lower caste students about their behaviour, language and mannerisms, and showed their biased attitudes towards caste. The policy of reservation has been such that, everyone criticizes and opposes it, but in private and informal discussions. I used to listen to them and try and get more and more information about their caste based biases and stereotypes. I did not reveal my caste. Gradually, they would come to know my caste identity through sources, and I could clearly see the difference in their interaction with me. They would slowly withdraw from me. It was very clear that I did not belong to the Brahmin caste. So one major categorization of a person is clear.Then it was difficult to label me as Maratha, OBC or SC as the surname is common across these caste categories. Some used to guess my caste on the basis of my language (Marathi), pronunciation and the accent; particularly the Maharashtrians. The second main point to dig out the caste label was the area/topic of research interest. Then I got labelled on caste lines being SC as my area of interest and the topic of my thesis had been the SCs. This used to result into forming the opinion and assuming that I belonged to the SC category without mentioning it. I would like to add that such were my experiences in JNU as well. And thus a person's calibre, intelligence and status would get determined; SCs being inferior in all these. The Indian mind in general keeps looking and digging for one's caste based on one's name, surname, locality one lives in, language one speaks, body language, appearance and sometimes the dress style. Those availing the reservation policy, instantly and categorically, are of the SC-ST category and are labelled as low backward and inferior with poor abilities.

I was the first SC on the faculty position who had entered

the TISS in 1984 along with a ST colleague. This fellow was Christian and had a different orientation altogether but was sensitive to such issues; showing activeness in all the matters pertaining to caste, discrimination, etc. Among the administrative staff, there were very few SC staff working at lower and middle level but were recruited in open competition. I am not sure of the ST staff. After I settled down after a few months, we the SC-ST faculty and staff started meeting informally more with feelings of oneness and solidarity. It was a medium to share and discuss problems. The ST colleague was also never appreciated in his department. Everyone in the Institute seemed apprehensive of the SC-ST issues. They hardly seemed to have any concern or sympathy towards the issues and they seemed to be biased against these communities. This can be attributed to their gross lack of awareness and lack of orientation and sensitization. This was certainly the moral and social responsibility of the premier Social Work institute that offers degrees in Social Work with the basic principles of equality and justice. I was very upset to see this gross violation of the policy of reservation and an atmosphere that was silent about it. I wondered, why the well known academician preceding director Dr. M.S. Gore was silent and why he ignored such a basic and important issue. After he retired, Dr. Armity Desai took over as Director of the institute and only after that the issue was taken up; by whom, why and how is not known to me exactly. They then started implementing the policy in the administration as well. This led to having a sizable number of the SC-ST employees. During the days, we the SC-ST employees had started thinking of formation of the SC-ST employees association with the intention of keeping solidarity and social security with proper implementation of the reservation policy, to fight for our rights against injustice. Finally, we formed the SC-ST Employees' Welfare

Association and got it registered with the governmrnt office and finally made an appeal to the Bombay High Court to order the TISS to implement the resevation policy and establish the SC-ST Cell which the TISS did.

The Balancing Act: Work and Family

Along with official responsibilities and long interrupted thesis work, I concentrated again on my thesis. There was no teaching responsibility. Since it was a research unit, the major focus used to be on sponsored research at national and international levels. The faculty members would develop a course and offer it to the social work students if one wished. The headship of the departments/units was not on rotation basis that time. So once your turn came you headed it till you retired or resigned from the position. I am thankful to Prof. Aikara, Prof. Hebsur and others for their cooperation and encouragement to complete my thesis. However, some or the other official responsibility would interrupt the thesis work in addition to my familial responsibilities. Radha by then came back with a baby girl. I was not able to concentrate more on the thesis. This was followed by my first visit to West Germany for three months under the DAAD exchange programme in 1990. After my return from Germany, I applied for study leave again that was sanctioned. Then I had nothing else to do than concentrate on the thesis work. With full concentration, I wrote a first draft and went to Delhi to discuss the draft with my guide. Thus I made three trips to Delhi and completed the thesis and finally submitted it towards the end of 1993. Six months after submission, the viva voce was conducted, which was a record in JNU since it usually took a year or two. At last, I was awarded the doctoral degree and I had fulfilled my ultimate dream in academics. JNU does not hold a convocation function for award of degrees like other universities. The awardees collect their certificates informally like any other administrative activity either in person or in absentia. I chose to receive it in absentia. Two months later, I received the certificate by post that was folded and stapled to a covering letter. I was surprised but remembered that the JNU administration was for slow functioning and carelessness. And yet, I am proud to have studied in JNU. It was a real turning point in my life with thorough academic and intellectual exposure. JNU taught me to question, to enquire, to listen, to talk, to argue, to do research and to expand my span of knowledge. Political understanding and maturity, ideological discourse, communism, socialism, capitalism and Amebedkarism—all of it I learned at JNU. It also gave me a national and international level of academic and political exposure. I must consider JNU to be like Cambridge and Oxford for me and all the others coming from similar backgrounds. I owe so much to JNU, to the faculty, students and the environment that has been alive, free and open. I must mention here that I have preserved the JNU student identity card, the bank pass book and the local transportation bus pass that gave concession to travel. Believe me, I never had imagined that I would earn so many degrees in my life: MA, BEd, MPhil and PhD. I am the first and the only person, not only in my own community in the village but also from other high caste communities to be educated up to this level (exceptionally, Radha's younger brother, Pradeep, has done very well academically. He has been a Ford Foundation Fellow and earned his PhD from the London School of Economics and Politics and is presently teaching at JNU. No doubt his achievements too are full of struggle). But sadly, even now, no one, except my elder brother, knows what these degrees mean, especially their value, level. I used to feel suffocated, both socially and intellectually due to my inability to convey and share such rare achievements and success with them. The routine possibilities were, otherwise to be a teacher at secondary school level and at the most, retire as headmaster of a school.

The Meeting of the Village and the World

On the office front by then I had completed a sponsored research project jointly with my colleague Jude Henrique on wastage and stagnation among the SCs and STs at school level. It was 1990 and I completed six years of service. But I could not complete my PhD thesis owing to several domestic and other problems. Also, my supervisor was far away in Delhi and I found it difficult to work and was prone to feeling demotivated. By chance, a colleague named Denzil Saldahna gave me the reference of Dr. Kalus Voll who was then the Ambassador for the West German Embassy in New Delhi. Dr. Voll was very sensitive socially, and a scholarly, active person with full knowledge of the worker community, child labour and poverty. I was encouraged by Denzil and Dr. Voll to apply for the DAAD fellowship under the faculty exchange programme. Denzil connected me to Professor Patrick Dias at the Department of Education, JW Goethe University, Frankfurt. Prof. Dias was a Goan settled in West Germany and consented to be my host in the department. I applied and got selected. This was a wonder for me as I had never even in my wildest dreams thought that I would go abroad. Everyone at home, in the village were very happy. After all the formalities and information, I decided to leave for Germany in July 1990 and started preparations including passport and then visa and other requirements. My brothers in Parbhani and Nanded gave news of my visit to Germany with my photograph in a local daily. For them it was a matter of great pride. Finally July appeared. The travel advance was drawn from the office. I went to the Air India office personally, thinking that it would be cheaper. However it was found to be more expensive compared to booking through a travel agent! I do not remember the exact date of departure. Father advised me not to travel by air because the plane might collapse any time and begged me to travel by train instead. Of course both father and mother knew nothing about my trip, its purpose, how far Germany is and all that. Finally the date of departure arrived. Both the brothers came to see me off. Everyone was happy. I was under tension whether I would be able to manage my journey and my stay in Germany; plus it was my first time travelling abroad and I was not sure what to carry along with me. At the same time I was worried about the children and Radha. The TISS sanctioned leave with pay under such provision for three months; so there was no worry financially. Finally on the day of departure, the flight was at 2 am, so we left home the previous night at 9.30 pm with my brothers in a private car that he had arranged. My younger brother greeted me at the airport with two garlands as a surprise! Before my check in, both of them put the garlands around my neck wishing me all the best. We were feeling very emotional; I touched my elder brother's feet and the younger touched mine. Finally I checked in saying goodbye to them and disappeared into the crowd of passengers. After the security check, I reached the check in counter, got my boarding pass and put in one bag in luggage. Waiting for the boarding announcement at 1 am, I felt the need to have tea because I was tired. There was no question of buying from the expensive restaurants where they accepted only US dollars. A boy was selling local tea with milk unofficially. I bought a cup of tea paying four times more than the regular cost. The entire environment inside was new, surprising and unbelievable with its richness, decorations with shops of all kinds with such expensive rates. I was thinking as to how and why people spend so much. For sometime, I forgot that I was in India. Such a sharp contradiction in the world inside the airport and outside. Finally, Air India made the boarding announcement for the Frankfurt flight and I stood in the boarding queue. Occupying the seat, I put my bags in the overhead locker and relaxed. My memories went into the past recalling my parents, their conditions, the village, my childhood, the hunger, the work as a child, the hardships of all types, caste discrimination, untouchability, etc. Suddenly I found my eyes full of tears and I was choked emotionally. This was unbelievable, unimaginable and yet the truth was that I was in the plane that would take me to Germany, away from my motherland, my culture and society that had always treated me like a second-class citizen, and hurt my dignity and respect in various inhuman ways. I had heard and read that in Western societies humans are not treated like this and have more individual freedom and dignity. It was a good opportunity to make a comparison and experience the difference between the two societies: western—modern and open versus eastern—closed and traditional in the modern days of the late 20th century. Even though the flight was full of passengers both Indian and foreigner, I was hesitant to speak to anyone. It was a new situation for me and I was feeling constricted and shy. The plane took off on time. It was almost a ten-hour journey. The drinks with dinner were served after an hour or so. I was so attracted by the movies they were screening on board that I kept watching and slept off without realizing. I woke up only after the plane landed at the Frankfurt airport late in the morning. Full of eagerness and enthusiasm, I completed all the formalities at the airport. Frankfurt was a huge and busy airport. Every four minutes a flight would land or take off. At the departure gate there were two persons waiting to receive me. One was a lady research staff of the education department and the gentleman was her boy friend: Hildegard and Tony. Both were tall and healthy. Tony took my big baggage and Hildegard took the small one. Tony shook hands and the lady shook hands and also gave me a welcome hug and kiss on my cheeks. This was a culture shock; a woman shaking hands and kissing the person she had just met. Certainly I did not forget this for three-four days and used to feel embarrassed and shy whenever I recall the moment. I always narrated this incident to the students in the class or at a public discourse in the appropriate situation. They drove me by car to the room they had rented for me. It was somewhat away from the main city, but it was a huge house with lush greenery and garden. The landlady lived in the house and had a grown up son. There was another African person staying as a tenant next to my room. We had a small common kitchen and bathroom. The room was booked through the University Department of Students' Welfare. Before occupying the room, I had to sign an agreement for three months with rent payment on a monthly basis. Surprisingly, the land lady used to speak English fluently. I was told the lady had been renting out rooms to the students for some time. However, after three-four days I realized that she was prejudiced against people of colour. Whenever I used to cook the Indian stuff I had carried, she would object and shout, yell and comment critically. The African friend also confirmed this to me. Somehow I managed for a month. I told this to Tony and Hildegard. They also confirmed things from others about the lady's behaviour. Well, in reality I was not surprised by this situation. Such elements are found everywhere in all societies. But never and nowhere like in India.

The education department was far from the main campus of the J.W. Goethe University. It was a private building rented out by the university. The place I stayed was far from the department. So I used to travel by local trains (Uban) every day. I knew no German and hence it used to be a problem to communicate; especially out of the university premises. Hildegard and Tony came to pick me up from my room on the first day. They introduced me to the professor Patric Dias, his colleagues and the secretary Ursula and the students. A student called Bernd Fetchler was given special responsibility to look after me. I was given a space to sit. Thus my routine began. After getting back home in the evening, I used to feel bored because there was no one to talk to and I felt lonely and missed my family, especially the children. The strangest thing to adjust to was the late sunset; it completely upset my local routine and affected my diet and sleep as well. The very first day of my stay I found that the sun was shining brightly at 9.30 pm. I asked the landlady who assured me that it was normal at this time of the year. However, because of summer, the weather was pleasant with greenery all over. The roads, gardens, houses and grounds, everything was neat and clean. The air was very fresh and clean. Overall, I found the Germans to be pleasant and cooperative people. They were tall, healthy and good looking people with sharp features. Sometimes I would get confused in identifying gender due to similarity in their looks and the long hair. Notably, they were very self-disciplined with respect for others and always spoke in a low voice. I hardly saw anybody running/rushing for a crowded bus or train. The population was very thin even in an international city like Frankfurt. My mind could not help but compare all that with the environment, cleanliness and public discipline in India.

The very first day I went to report to the DAAD scholarship holders department of the university with Hildegard, and I was paid the scholarship's first instalment instantly with no enquiry whatsoever.

Hildegard used to visit me on and off and Bernd used to visit at my place of stay regularly. Both of them were familiar with Indian culture because Hildegard was doing her PhD work on Tamil Nadu and knew Tamil to some extent. Bernd had visited Bangalore under a youth programme. He had joined the diploma course in education after willingly dropping out from the MBBS course. Once I was feeling very homesick and had a cold and body pain. I called Bernd and asked him to bring me medicine and some fruit. He felt bad hearing my voice on the telephone and asked me why I was speaking so harshly as if I was ordering him. He got me medicine and fruit, but I got very emotional feeling homesick. He consoled me and I asked for his forgiveness. Actually it was my routine way of speaking as an Indian. This is in great contrast to how they speak softly in a low voice unlike Indians. I always found it difficult to follow their style of speaking. By then I had picked up three-four sentences of German. I could meet the professor after his return from the World Sociological Conference in Spain. The landlady's attitude was unchanging though, and consequently Tony suggested that I shift to his house and pay a lower rate of rent as his house lay vacant since he cohabited with Hildegard at a different place. Tony managed to convince the landlady to forgo the contract under the pretext that I needed to go to different places for research work. Thus, after a month I shifted to the new house with two rooms with other required facilities.

So Ursula, Hildegard and Bernd, one of the three always used to meet, enquire and help me. They would take me around the city, to some music or movie shows and museums. After the evening however I used to feel lonely and bored. There was nobody to talk to. Even if you went out for a walk or visit a garden, you could not talk to anyone like in India. This is merely an observation about German culture, lifestyle and traditions and not a criticism.

The professor organized my lecture on education of SC-ST in India at the department. It was attended by students, faculty members and a few local Indians who had settled in Germany. I clearly noticed a thing that everybody there takes the lecture, teaching, discussion and topic seriously and listens to you attentively. If anything is not clear, they will ask you questions till they are satisfied. Academics is taken seriously with due respect with special respect to the profession. Teaching is respected in its true sense. Once while walking on the road, I asked the way to a German lady, of course in English. The lady said "No English, speak in German." I politely told her I do not know German. "What are you doing in Germany if you do not know German?" she retorted. I was taken aback and did not know what to say. I told her I was from India and knew English which is common due to colonial rule and that I studied through English and I was a teacher at a university and had come to Germany under the DAAD exchange programme based in the Education Department. The lady was happily surprised and changed her tone and very respectfully appreciated while bowing her head. Wishing me the best, she went ahead. I sincerely felt very happy with my heart full of gratitude for my profession. Then I asked myself: do I get the same respect and gratitude in my own country for my profession? I experienced this respect and gratitude everywhere during my stay. This used to give me complete satisfaction and feelings of pride in my profession. In Germany one finds all sorts of museums:

historical, animals, war, botany, paintings and so on. Each and every museum is well maintained with entry fees. I visited a few selected ones because it was expensive for me. In those days the country had the German mark as currency and was very expensive when converted to Indian rupees. I was very careful in spending money and always used to convert and count in rupees. Sometimes it used to frustrate me if the money was spent on useless things. Once Bernd took me to an international musical concert that was organized in the largest garden in Frankfurt city. I did not enjoy the show at all because I knew nothing about Western music. After some time, we had tea and snacks and I asked Bernd to leave the show; so we left half way. Bernd was staying alone in a rented room; studying and doing odd jobs to earn. Once he invited me on his birthday. There I met many people including his parents and friends. He introduced me to everyone. While introducing me to his parents he said, "meet my mother and her boy friend and meet my father and his girl friend." He went on introducing his friends and their beloveds. I found no one married. Some of them were carrying babies too. It was a shock for me to witness such relations including the boy and girlfriend of the father and mother. Bernd had also recently broken up with his girlfriend. We had an enjoyable party with drinks and dinner till late at night. However, surprisingly, there were no cheers, wishes and songs, no birthday cake and candle on this occasion. What could be the reason? I used to be a silent observer with no judgments; good or bad. I witnessed similar things on the birthday of Tony, Hildegard and others. I tried to ask and know as to why they did not cut cake and light the candle with birth day songs. No one could give me a satisfactory answer. One more such birthday celebration I attended was that of Bernd's new girl friend. We went to her house quite early. She was staying with a girl partner. Bernd and I helped her to clean the entire house. By evening many others joined us. Bernd bought a full carton of wine, beer and whisky and many types of ready food. The party began in the same way. There was a lady with a small baby, maybe of three-four years and an infant hanging around her neck. During the party I saw the baby drinking wine from a bottle. I brought it to the notice of Bernd. He told me it was normal and I was not to worry. Again it was a shock for me. I casually asked the mother about the age of the infant. She told me that it was 15 days old. The lady was drinking and eating everything. It was an open space in the nearby garden. This was another shock to me. I remembered our birthday celebrations and the dos and don'ts we follow when it comes to a mother with a fifteen-day infant. Bernd had confided that his girlfriend was sexually exploited by her father. Now knowing this too, Bernd accepted her as his girl friend. What do we call this? An open society? Advanced society? Or a society with no norms? It is a great thing to appreciate that Bernd could share that with me openly with no hesitation. What I admire is the openness, boldness and honesty they have with each other.

By now Bernd was quite close to me as a friend. He used to take care of me in every way. Those were the days of large-scale migration of refugees from East European countries after the collapse of the Soviet Union. Also there was a heavy influx of people migrating to West Germany from East Germany. The Berlin Wall had been destroyed just a few months back in 1990 and the unification of Germany was officially declared. In effect, a large number of youth were seen everywhere in a free and open society as against the restrictive communist rule in their countries. The city of Frankfurt and Berlin were more crowded due to these migrants. They found everything new, the shops, the markets, restaurants, gardens and the malls. Everything was open freely and enjoyable. At times I would spot young boys stealing things from shops and malls and getting caught on CCTV and then facing the law and punishments. I noticed that they would show curiosity about sex shops that were as new to them as they were for me. With great hesitation and reluctance I also used to hang around and peep into such shops; it being just a wonder and a shock. I was not able to understand as to why the government allowed this to show and sell so openly. On one day a group of young boys and girls from Poland was to visit Frankfurt under the sponsorship of the Church and Bernd was given responsibility as the host. Bernd took them around the city visiting several places. Of course I was part of them. But could not speak to them at all due to the language problem. In the evening he hosted a dinner for them at his residence. It was a drinks and dinner party. I reached the venue slightly late. I was helping Bernd in arranging things. The party went on till late night with loud music. Finally each one slept wherever they found a place. I slept in a corner. Towards morning, I felt something warm and soft touch my bed and felt odd. I checked it and to my wonder it was a young girl sleeping in deep sleep snoring loudly. I lost my sleep because of discomfort, wondering how a young girl could sleep in the bed of a man with such a fearless mind. This incident is still fresh in my mind. It is certainly a matter of perceptions and pre-conceived notions. Similarly I was witness to other birthday parties like that of Hildegard, Tony and others with calm, simple celebrations without much show and expenses. No hotel, no resort or pub, they occurred just at home.

I cannot forget the person called an Indian-Marathi-Dalit research scholar who had been living in Frankfurt for

20 years at that time (I suppose he is still there) for his PhD. During those times he was granted a visa for a long period. He met me during my lecture at the department. He was a warm person with a supportive nature and kind heart. He was socially aware and concerned about Dalit issues. We engaged in long discussions on Dalits and their problems in India. He invited me to his huge rented house for dinner a few times and served Indian food. He was living with his Indian wife and two small sons. He and his wife both worked on a part-time basis which was more than enough to live a good quality life. The other Muslim couple I met was from Bangladesh. They also had a similar history of education, job and family. I was also invited to dinner by them. Most of the people from Asia I met during my stay were mainly from India, Pakistan and Bangladesh. They were all very cordial, helpful with strong feelings of solidarity. In no way did I experience difference or distance in them. I was wondering why the same people think and behave negatively with each other in their own country. Maybe it was because of the foreign land and culture; being away from their motherland that makes them so pleasant. Honestly speaking, I used to be apprehensive about students who were from Pakistan, maybe out of an inherent bias.

Once I met a German lady at a function. She insisted on me visiting her home at Marburg that is a one hour journey from Frankfurt. One fine day her partner happened to come to Frankfurt. He came to my place and took me to Marburg. They had a child but were not married. I stayed with them at their home overnight. They treated me so warmly with dinner and took me around the town and some farm fields. Marburg is a globally-known town for training and manufacturing goods for the handicapped. There are signals with music tones on the road for the blind to cross. I was impressed by the social inclusiveness of the town and felt elevated by my hosts' warm treatment.

Academically, I was interested to know more about the social life, culture and education in Germany. Once I visited a school in Frankfurt with the help of Hildegard. After I introduced myself, I could easily see that the principal and teachers were both seen to be unwelcoming. I expressed my wish to sit and observe the class. I was denied permission to enter the classroom. After some time, I left the school with utter dissatisfaction. I remembered when these people visited India for research, every Indian ran after them with all possible support and hospitality besides all kinds of academic support. I was not sure of the reason behind not allowing me to sit in the class and observe. The issue of guest workers has been a major issue in German politics and academics. I used to witness this everywhere, in the university, among the scholars and students. I was very curious about and had developed an interest to read and listen to accounts about this subject. The guest workers are the ones who were invited to work and rebuild Germany after the Second World War; they were mainly from Turkey. During those times many of them settled in Germany. They must have been third generation immigrants at the time of my visit. They were distinctly different from the Germans. The majority of them were Muslims and their language was different from Germans. They lived in separate localities that were specially developed for them. So the issues like their identity, culture, education and citizenship besides wages were the core issues for debate. They were not yet accepted by the locals and treated as second class citizens in general. However, there were sections of people supporting their cause; many activists and NGOs were working for them. One such lady activist happened to be the Labour Minister then. She was a strong lady with leadership qualities. Hildegard suggested that I should meet her. She made an appointment for me and accompanied me to meet her. In our very brief meeting, she gave me information and some material on the guest workers and was very supportive of them. I was trying to compare these social realities of identity crisis and discrimination with the Dalits of India. I tried to meet some of the students and youngsters and had discussions on the issue. The younger generation was more comfortable because they were born there and knew the German language. The older ones complained of the discrimination and distance. Language was a problem as they did not know English and I did not know either German or their language. After my return, I had decided to write an article and publish but somehow could not do so and during the course of time lost all the material. This makes me more certain of the fact that discrimination is everywhere but in different forms with different bases. In this case I was not sure whether it was on the basis of race or religion or language and/or because of their low status as workers. It will be interesting to do a research study on the issue after the gap of a quarter century to know the situation.

Like Hildegard, there was a German scholar Joel (not sure of name), who was in India for research on the DAAD scholarship. He was doing data collection in West Bengal. I met him at a seminar that was organized by Dr. Voll at Jilling near Dehradun. He was a Berliner, very socially sensitive probably because he belonged to the working class. I have been in touch with him and I wrote a letter to him from Frankfurt. He invited me to Berlin instantly. Distance between the two cities is quite a lot. Travelling expenses were out my reach so Hildegard suggested that a shared car was cheaper. It was like this: any person travelling a long distance would book the travel date and time and the destination at the office of the agent who would coordinate with the owner of the vehicle and the person who wanted to travel to the same destination. Both had to pay reasonable charges to the agent and then the passenger would pay officially fixed charges to the vehicle owner. Accordingly, Hildegard took me to the agent's office and paid the charges. I chose the date and time for travel as per the car owner's time and date. On the given date and time, a lady came to pick me up. We began the journey to Berlin. She spoke broken English. She was a pleasant person who addressed me respectfully. It was, I think a journey of 500 kilometres or so. We halted at a spot for tea and while filling the petrol she asked me to pay the petrol charges. There was no staff at the petrol pump. Everything was done with automatic machines. This was another surprise for me. Most of things were done by machines for human services. The road was clean and wide. Every vehicle ran with full discipline and adherence to rules. That was my first time of travelling with a woman with such high speed. At times I used to feel scared of the speed and doubt her skills and capacity of driving being a woman. Ironically, this was 1990. Finally she dropped me at the exact location. We said goodbye to each other with thanks. I must reiterate that there was no question of cheating and bargaining; every law and rule was followed strictly. My friend had asked his lady friend to receive me and entertain me as he was at work in an old age home. This was his part-time job and compulsory under the law as social service as an alternative to military service that is compulsory for all youth up to a certain age for a minimum of two years. The lady received me warmly and took me to the room that was ready for me. She knew a smattering of English. After some time she came to my room with a tray full of tea and snacks. I presumed she was his wife, but luckily I did not speak about it. This was in a complex of multiple buildings built for and by the poor and working people with an initiative of a few social activists. This friend of mine was one of the people responsible for developing this complex with the help of a government grant. He told me later that he himself was working in the construction task with other people. He introduced me to many people there. We used to have good discussions on various issues, particularly on India. We visited several sites, the old parliament, museums and the famous Berlin theatre and the spot where Hitler was hiding in a bunker and then killed himself. The city has several buildings that were bombed during the Second World War which were very well preserved as memories. The visit to East Berlin city made me know the difference between dictatorship and democracy and its impact on people, culture and development. It was a poor show of Russian power and communism. The friend one fine morning took me to the site of the Berlin Wall that was demolished a months ago. There were some remains of the wall and people were collecting small cement stones of the wall as a memory. I picked up one and brought it home; however it was lost during the course of time. There was a board with names painted of those who were killed or died during the efforts for crossing the wall from East to West city. It was a major setback to the people of Germany; first due to the world wars and the genocide of Jews and then the communist regime. All these historical events, political dictatorship and racial supremacy had an impact on the entire world and humanity. Yet another site that gave me a big surprise was the memorial of the homosexuals that were killed by Hitler. The memorial is built with a tall pillar with names of all those who were killed. The city of Berlin also has a significant number of guest workers and many activists are fighting for their cause. I also visited and had some interactions with the faculty at the Free University of Berlin and the Education Department of the famous Max Plank Institute. It was time to leave for Frankfurt after a seven days stay in Berlin. The host friend booked the share car for me and I left for Frankfurt thanking him and all the others who helped and entertained me with their warm hospitality. Before leaving, I ate the roasted beef at the shop owned by a Turkish man. It was half roasted and heavy for digestion. It spoiled my digestion and I had a stomach pain during the entire journey. One thing special I noticed in Germany was nobody ever talks of Hitler and the war. I tried to ask questions and information about many things such as Hitler, the war and genocide. They used to avoid my questions or directly decide not to talk about the issue. They also said that they did not know about Hitler's graveyard and its location. One can guess the reason for this. One more thing related to the Second World War was the military camps of the friendly countries existing till date all over and yet things were going smoothly. It must be interesting to know their history books in education and what they teach their students on the wars and related issues. However, it is worth recording the development this country made in all the fields, especially technology despite total breakdown and complete destruction due to the Second World War. India got freedom almost at the same time and could not even attain half the progress of Germany. Is it because of their work culture, national commitment, diligence, dignity of labour and human values? One could scientifically probe into this area of the post war situation and the development, both material and non-material. Why is it called a developed country even after having had a complete breakdown?

I reached Frankfurt late at night and was not able to give the correct home address to the car owner. This was due to the language problem. He drove the car all around the locality to drop me as he was supposed to do that officially. Finally I gave him the landlady's phone number, which I was avoiding knowing that she would scream at that time. He called her and got the exact address. He dropped me home and only then went away. Following rules and human safety were the prime focus. I say this because of my own experiences as a foreigner in the country having lived there for three months. I think it is enough time to observe and experience things and form opinions.

Another gentleman I met was Mr. Vijay Kumar who was from South India. Initially he went to Germany to study engineering and then married a German woman and settled there with a job. He was very active socially. Once he invited Hildegard and me for dinner. I reached early as a precaution to avoid delay. But I was delayed. The delay happend due to the language problem. All the road directions and sign boards were in German. Vijay Kumar's wife received me at his home. She spoke to me in good English, while Mr. Vijay Kumar was busy cooking Indian food. After some time, Hildegard got there with a bottle of wine. I felt bad because I did not bring a bottle of wine or beer because I did not realize it since we in India do not have such a practice in general. I had a good and rare opportunity of having Indian food. We all had an enjoyable dinner and I left thanking them after some time. Each time, everyone was so curious about India, and its social issues like caste, untouchability, poverty, education and politics. Some Indians, like students and those settled there, were unhappy and reluctant to talk about such problems thinking that it brought a bad name to India. One wonders as to why and how it brings a bad name if one discusses realities; especially when it is an academic discourse.

By this time I had finished a month of my stay in Germany. I was missing home. Those days only telephone facilities and the postal services were available for communication. I used to write letters to my elder brother and call Radha on our neighbour's phone. To have a landline at home was a luxury and a very expensive thing in those days. So calling home was restricted due to expenses and using the neighbour's phone. Once, Hildegard's lady friend happened to visit Mumbai. She was known to Denzil. I took the opportunity to buy toys and requested her to give them to my children in Mumbai. She was glad to oblige. She gave them to Denzil who passed them on to Radha. I felt privileged to give such good foreign toys to my children when I do not remember ever playing with a single toy during my childhood. In my time, if parents possessed some skill and could spare time, they would make dolls out of rags.

I shifted to Tony's house. The house was located in a locality close to the tower that was known for its height and a huge ground nearby. It was the time for general elections in Germany. All the candidates, men and women contesting elections used to visit people and localities freely and openly without any special security arrangements and ask for votes. There were a few sitting ministers in the group too. It was surprising for me to see such cordial and peaceful election propaganda with no big rallies, shows, slogans, banners and loudspeakers unlike elections in India. This was in a democracy for parliamentary elections with only two parties: Liberal and Conservative. One of the major issues for the election was that of garbage being created out of tissue papers. By now I had finished all the tobacco I had carried and switched to cigarettes. One fine morning while walking to a cigarette shop, I saw a big TV set dumped away. Tony mentioned it was more expensive to repair electronic items so people disposed of things like that. I did not have a TV at home that time as it was a luxury item for me. When I reached the cigarette shop there was a queue for buying them. On the way back, I almost had a car accident. They have right side traffic rules as against left side as in India and it is difficult to remember. Often I used to fumble, get confused or lose confidence or board the wrong bus or Uban. This was happening firstly due to the language problem and secondly, due to unfamiliarity with advanced technology. One had to buy a bus ticket at the stop that had an auto machine to buy a ticket with a map and the fare indicated. As a result, I used to feel bad and frustrated due to my inability to adopt and adjust to the realities. But at the same time I felt proud and fortunate to be abroad and have a new exposure and rare experiences in life.

Ursula took me for outing two-three times with her car and treated me lavishly. I was wondering how she could afford to spend so much money on me. Later I came to know that there is a provision of some amount with the fellowship to entertain scholars/visitors. What a wonder! Bernd of course entertained me always at his home or out with his friends. Once he took me to watch a movie. After the show we had some snacks. While having snacks, I saw a big board in front of a building advertising a "gay club"and asked him to go and have a look. He advised me not to go because it would then create a problem for both of us since it was a gay club. It was another culture shock for me. I wondered what one could call it: an advanced human culture or symbol of a free and open society or a by product of modernity.

Looking at my academic interest in the guest workers

problem, I was advised by Hildegard and others to visit the UNICEF office in Paris for more information. I was also keen to visit Paris, but did not have a visa for France. All of them advised me to try for a visa from the consulate in Frankfurt city. The professor at the department gave me a supporting letter explaining the need to visit the UNICEF office. Next day I went to the French consulate and filled in the application for a visa. The officer called me and plainly refused to grant a visa saying that the visa had to be obtained from the mother country. I decided however to take a chance and persuaded her with academic reasons. Then she asked me to produce the return tickets to Mumbai which I did. She then asked me to come back the next day. I went without much hope, but was delighted to know that I had been granted the visa. I subsequently travelled by train to Paris and stayed in a youth hostel. My stay in France came with its own set of challenges. The first was locating the hostel because of unfamiliarity with the French language. Next day I went to the UNICEF office and met the concerned department and got the required material including their reports for my work. Thanking the official, I then went around the beautiful city for two-three days. I visited the Louvre museum and saw the famous Monalisa painting, the Eiffel tower and so on. I cannot emphasize enough my feeling of joy and my good fortune. On the way back to Frankfurt on the fifth day, I went to the tourists' guidance desk at the Paris railway station to ask about the train and platform. The lady refused to speak in English. And this was common in Paris: the refusal to speak in English. I wonder what could be the reasons behind this. Was it out of dislike for English or out of historical dislike of the English people? Or was it an outcome of traditional feelings of English-French rivalry? After all, Paris is an international spot.

On the way back to Frankfurt, I boarded a train in the morning. There were two-three passengers sitting next to my seat. One appeared to be Indian by his appearance and skin colour. Another fellow was European but I could not make out his country. After the initial conversation it was found that one was of Indian origin from Pondicherry and had French citizenship and was running a cloth business. The other person was German. Being Indian, I initiated more conversation asking his name and other primary details. To my surprise he knew only Tamil and French while I knew neither. More surprisingly, the German fellow opted to translate French into English for me. And thus we three enjoyed the journey till Frankfurt. The world is so big and yet so small too! This was an eye-opener for me. Non-English European developed countries have also developed their own language; their education, science, technology, etc. While I had been taught to believe that modern knowledge is available only in English.

During the three month stay, I met students, teachers, artists, etc. from various countries including Indians. Some of them were from Pakistan and Bangladesh. One Pakistani student was close to me. He was doing a part-time job like many others. All those who did not know German had to compulsorily do a six month course in the language. This Pakistani friend did the course in addition to knowing German well. He also had a German girl friend and stayed in a student hostel. Once he took me to his hostel which had both male and female residents. They also shared the wash room. This fellow with his other Pakistani friend cooked a delicious Pakistani dinner with rotis and beef. We had dinner together. I stayed in his room for the night. In the morning I was absolutely alarmed to see a woman in the bathroom. She had just come out from the toilet. I was to go for toilet use but was feeling very reluctant and strange to use it in her presence. Somehow I managed and I asked the friend about it. He just laughed. He explained that it was quite normal for men and women to share everything including bathrooms. I could not get over the fact that both male and female students were living in such a manner.

By now I had got used to the the lifestyle to some extent. It was the beginning of October and winter. Luckily the house I was staying in was centrally heated; for that matter every house is centrally heated in Germany. Then it was time for me to pack up and leave for my motherland. I was very desperate and excited to go back home. I think it was the third week of October. I started preparations and shopped carefully with the limited money I had. I bought toys for Shweta and Vikrant and a sari for Radha (that she did not like and wore just twice and finally gave to the maid) from an Indian shop owned by a Punjabi. Punjabis were in a majority among Indians there; some lived illegally. They are hard working doing all kinds of jobs like cleaning cars and houses and some do business like running restaurants, shops with Indian goods. Once I had dinner at a Punjabi restaurant and he did not accept money from me with great feelings of respect and appreciation being Indian. I did not buy anything for myself to save money thinking my trip itself was a great gift for me. I got busy in leaving of the people whom I had met and who had helped me. I must honestly express apologies to a young German who was fond of Indian music and had given me 100 German marks to buy and send him a *tabla* after I reached India: a request that I could not somehow fulfil.

On the day of my departure, I was excited to go back home. My brothers came to Mumbai to receive me. They waited at the exit gate till midnight. Finally, after all clearances I emerged to be received with garlands. After the customary feet-touching, (a custom that is slowly disappearing today) we all travelled home in a rented car. It was early morning 6 am. Radha and the children were waiting for us at home.

Interactions with Students

The teaching profession is considered to be a noble profession across the world. India has a great tradition of knowledge, teaching—learning but limited to the particular upper caste, especially Brahmins till recently. It is the colonial rule in India that introduced modern education and was open to everyone in principle. However, the first beneficiary castes of this modern education of course were the upper castes and in particular the Brahmins, by virtue of the social and cultural capital they enjoyed historically and traditionally. However, in the case of lower castes that form the majority of the population, it took longer for them to access modern education; the untouchables took even longer due to their pathetic social and economic conditions and educational deprivation. The late 18th and the beginning of the 19th century was the landmark period in India's educational history. One can identify the major factors responsible for this major reshuffling in education such as the role of Christian missionaries, modern knowledge and skills required to run the government and the military services needed for defence. And one can also add the overall policy and positive attitude of British rule towards the Indian downtrodden. It was the Church, for the first time in history, that was open to the untouchables. British officials were the first to employ the untouchables as domestic servants. This was supported in a big way by the Indian social reformers who were products of English education and who took up various social issues like caste, untouchability and education. Jyotiba Phule, Savitribai Phule, Prince Shau Maharaj, Prince Sayaji Gaikwad and

Dr. B.R. Ambedkar are the landmark examples. After independence, India adopted the constitution that focuses on equality, justice and fraternity and provided several measures for uplifting all the downtrodden including the untouchables (SCs now) due to Dr. Ambedkar's concerted efforts. It is in this context that both formal teaching and learning activities need to be understood.

Traditionally and historically the Brahmins had monopoly in the profession of teaching and running educational institutions and in many ways it continues even today. However, the dichotomy between demand and supply of knowledge could not resist the monopoly. At the same time 'teaching' slowly turned out to be more a form of employment. The Affirmative Action Policy implemented since the mid 20th century opened the gates of 'teaching' but more as a job that leads to social and economic mobility. To be a teacher at university level has been more prestigious as compared to be at school or college level. Frankly speaking, I got into this job as faculty at the central university more out of compulsion than choice and also out of chance; it happened exactly when I was badly in need of a job to earn money.

I must honestly say that I had a basic liking and aptitude for teaching. My teacher training degree (BEd.) helped me sharpen my teaching skills and added an appreciation for teaching. I began as a school teacher for an academic year soon after I completed the BEd. and that was, again to say, out of financial compulsions. At the TISS I found it to be a mix of discomfort and enjoyment as a faculty with students and fellow colleagues. This could be firstly, because of the social and educational background I came from and secondly, the fact that the appointment was under reserved quota which invited open or subtle stereotypes and biases against me. All this finally resulted into some seen/unseen limitations while interacting with students. These students in a majority then were invariably from the urban middle class and castes with an English educational background. I used to openly see and feel their difficulties in relating to me or accepting me as a teacher in the class and outside class. On the contrary, students coming from rural/poor and vernacular (mostly by virtue of reservation policy) used to feel closer, open and expressive. Was it because they and I both came from the same social and cultural background? Or was it due to a common social identity? I taught the course, 'Indian Education System: Issues and Strategies for Social Workers' for many years. The example I used to cite in the class used to be mostly from a real rural milieu with problems such as poverty, casteism, discrimination, untouchabilty, patriarchy, etc. Many of them were reluctant to accept these; to the extent of refusing to accept that there is caste and casteism, untouchability or poverty in India. This fault could be attributed to the education system, the teacher, the course contents, the pedagogy or the society by and large. How much it is relevant and necessary to unlearn while learning! Do academic excellence and knowledge really come from intelligence and a particular social background? Contradictorily, I found students coming from a rural, poor and socially deprived background to be more sensitive, hard working and having considerable potential to grow intellectually and academically. They had more patientce, tolerance and resistance power. May be these qualities were inherited from their long struggle for survival at individual, family and community levels. This is with no bias against others. In reality, what these students need is acceptance, sensitivity, moral and extra academic support with empathy. As and when I tried to explain in the class in Marathi/Hindi, as they used to understand better and add many points with examples from real life. The tragedy with Indian teachers is, generally they keep a wide distance from students, do not encourage them to argue, discuss or debate inside and outside the classroom. They are generally treated with preconceived notions of caste, gender, religion or language. All that finally results in poor performance and weak skills. I always encouraged/allowed students to meet me personally/privately in the office room or elsewhere and share their problems; be it health-related, emotional, academic, financial or familial. Many of them used to open up fully and express their anger, frustration, expectations and even their very personal/private problems and feel unburdened and relieved. Many used to cry literally out of helplessness. Sometimes I tried to help them by giving study material or limited financial support from my personal means. At the same time, I always tried to be strict at academic and administrative levels, follow all the rules religiously and help students within the rules. Some of them used to misunderstand me for not helping with things that were not right or against the rules. I would always keep correcting them over language, modern Western mannerisms, their approach to teachers and administrative staff. This was mainly due to clash of cultures: rural versus urban, traditional versus modern, English versus mother tongue. I have been happy and fully satisfied due to all this as I tried to remedy what I suffered and faced during my studentship.

Whenever I recall my experiences with students as a teacher and look for outcomes, I feel satisfied and also proud of them. They listened to me and implemented many things in their academic, social and personal lives. Many of them pursued further studies in India and abroad, many of them achieved higher positions in government jobs and also started NGOs serving deprived ones, despite coming from slums, remote villages and tribal areas. I consider this as my achievement and a rich, truly satisfying source of inspiration as a teacher. Although there were a few experiences of frustration and dissatisfaction, I have no regrets whatsoever.

The Dye is Cast

In 1994, I completed ten years of service. During this period I also completed two research projects and taught a course on 'Indian Education System: Issues and Strategies' for social workers. However, the faculty of the Unit could develop a course and teach after approval of the Academic Council. The course I taught for six-seven years was taught by a colleague who left the institute. It was discontinued later because the Institute made major changes in its academic structure. I was happy to teach because I liked teaching very much. My experiences while teaching this course are mixed; good and bad at academic and social levels. Good, because students used to enjoy my method of teaching and the content with its real examples from society and life. Being an optional course, it was taken mostly by students from a rural and vernacular background and particularly from SC-ST communities. Those from the urban middle class and upper castes with English/convent educated backgrounds would feel strange about the issues I used to deal with and find the examples strange and unknown. Hence sometimes I used to get into arguments with them. This was natural and justifiable because they had never been exposed to rural life and the problems related to poverty, caste, gender and discrimination in the education system of India. However, surprisingly, many students told me that their department faculty used to discourage or disallow them from opting for this course. The reasons can be guessed by using common sense. I was much aggrieved by this attitude, but could do nothing about it. After all it is the mindset of the people: whether it was a workplace or educational institution or the neighbourhood or the community or temple or any function—caste is always operative, openly or subtly. Dr. Ambedkar said in his book *Annihilation of Caste* that the seeds of wild grass are seen nowhere but they exist everywhere, similarly caste is not seen everywhere but exists everywhere. There are sections of Indians who say no caste exists now and yet another lot says that caste is there but there is no casteism any more. While another section believes that caste is everywhere causing harm to humans in many ways. I wish to put such people in the following categories—1. The sections of people who have immensely benefited out of the caste system for ages (the Brahmins and other upper castes). This section is small at the top of the social structure. 2. Another section is that of the victims of the caste system. These are in a majority but the degree of victimisation increases depending on the lower social level of caste in the structure, for example all backward/artisan casetes. 3.Those who have been fully victimized for ages with a social stigma and are at the bottom but not in the same scale of caste order (former untouchables). In reality, despite formal-informal efforts to eradicate caste and constitutional provisions and the modernization process, caste continues to exist both publicaly and privately when it comes to benefits and opportunities in terms of holding property, land, politics, marriage and inter-dining, barring a few exceptions in metro cities at special and public discourses. Apparently no one would dare to admit that he/she believes in the caste system and untouchability but invariably and conveniently would practise it. One could easily identify the major and visible broad indicators of caste, i.e. high or middle or low, with stigma, such as name and surname, residence and locality, language, body language and dress style. The educated class remains silent or talks/writes only superficially about the caste system to the extent that many believe caste is no more an issue.

Since a PhD was mandatory for higher position and there was no reservation at Reader and Professor level, it took ten years for me to be a Reader. Accordingly, I applied for the Reader's position. It is not based on the number of years of service but on one's teaching, research and publications. In addition one has to face a personal interview with eminent experts of the subject. I got selected for the position and thus earned the second highest position in academics. Within one year's time Rawat Publishers published my PhD thesis. The book is dedicated to my parents. This was my first independent full phased major publication. I also completed a few research projects for the Government of India and a few articles in journals. Based on this, I applied for a Professor's position against an advertisement in the Unit for Child and Youth Research (UCYR) where I got selected. Luckily, the selection procedure and the experts have been quite fair. I joined the new unit in TISS as Professor and Head, leaving the Sociology of Education unit and the colleagues who were supportive to me.

An incident that hurt my self-respect the most and demoralized me deeply needs to be mentioned here. I was then at the lecturer's position. It was in 1996, the Institute was celebrating its Diamond Jubilee week. Various academic activities and cultural programmes were organized. Everyone, including admin staff was given responsibility except me. I was wondering why so, but could not say anything to anyone. One such programme was organized to invite Mr. Daya Pawar, an eminent Dalit poet and author of *Baluta* to speak and have an open interview. After he arrived on the given day and time there was no one available to entertain him till the programme began. Then, a colleague in charge called me to go and entertain him. I went and spent time with him till he joined the stage. I wonder as to why I was not given any major or minor responsibility during such an event and why was I asked to entertain Daya Pawar. Was it because both of us happened to be Dalits or something else? I would call it a matter of bias or thought of taking me for granted or the mind that functions to differentiate from others. Such experiences have been many from students, colleagues and the admin staff. In the class, in the meetings, at the events, over discussions I would be singled out; as if I was a parasite for them. Several times colleagues would talk, and students and other staff would say things about me, my social identity, my calibre that is linked to fluent English speaking and inclined to sophisticated Westernized behaviour, qualities that I did not have. Their richness of social and cultural capital was inherited from parents and community: they received it without any efforts and struggle as it was made readily available. This is how the entire academic and intellectual community in India is enjoying status and prestige and continues to dominate from traditional to modern means of power, be it social, economic or cultural.

After reaching the high level of position, it was binding to be representing all important committees including selection committee and finally, towards the end of the service, as a representative of the SC-ST, I became a member of the Governing Board of the Institute which is a supreme body in policy making and taking important decisions. The Governing Board was a fair and non-interfering body appointed for the smooth functioning of the institute. The committees generally function in a fair and democratic manner but in the absence of basic awareness and direct concern, there has to be a constant persuasion, reminders and check when it comes to the issues of SC-ST, reservation policy and all related matters. However, overall administration was found to be fair and impartial barring a few exceptions. In fact, it was much better than any other university in the country.

By now all the teaching and non-teaching SC-ST staff had proved to be a pressure group for overall cohesive environment and social integration. But in some or the other way the issue of discrimination and deprivation used to come up either from students, staff or faculty who belonged to the SC-ST categories. One such major issue is worth mentioning. It was related to a research project involving some oil company to evaluate the environment effect. The project was done jointly by two faculty members, one a senior professor belonging to the Brahmin community and the other, a lecturer who belonged to the SC community. Towards the end, while writing the report, the lecturer refused to manipulate the data in the interest of the funding agency. Over this, the professor got so angry that he openly and loudly abused the lecturer making derogatory remarks about his caste. The lecturer felt so humiliated and insulted that with a trembling body he went to another faculty who belonged to the upper caste and was supposedly sympathetic to the SC-ST cause. Finally the next day he lodged an FIR under the Atrocity Act and the police came with the arrest warrant. The professor absconded, rather was helped to do so for two-three months to avoid the arrest. Finally, the case went to the criminal court. This continued for a few months. Unfortunately after six months or so the complainant suddenly died of brain haemmorhage while on the data collection in his own state of Uttar Pradesh. Despite the agitation launched by the SC-ST staff members and students on the campus for arrest of the professor, others on the campus tried to shield him from getting arrested. Finally after everything cooled down the professor quietly came to the office and started attending it regularly. The story ended with nothing and everyone was happy.

Academic Profile and the Profession

In all I completed 30 major research projects out of which two were international and nearly 22 for the Government of India against the ministries' invitation, mostly evaluation of various schemes and programmes meant for supporting education of weaker sections and gave relevant recommendations based on primary data. However, I hardly see any such recommendations accepted and implemented except for study on post matric scholarships meant for SC-ST, that too only a slight increase in the scholarship amount and income limit. In addition, I also published articles in various books and international journals mainly in the area of education of the SCs, particularly higher education. The UKIERI (United Kingdom-India Educational Research Initiative) was a major international research project led by me in India and Prof. Mary Thornton in the UK. I had fruitful interactions with the core team consisting of Prof. Ivan Reid, Dr. Patricia Bricheno, Dr. Roger Green and Ms. Ponni Iyer. The report was submitted to the British Council and the governments of both the countries and published by TISS. Internationally, I participated in various conferences/seminars held in Germany, South Africa, UK, China, Italy, Australia, and presented papers mainly on education of SCs. I also delivered lectures at Cambridge, Oxford, London School of Economics and Politics, Luxembourg, Bradford University, Paris besides visits to Switzerland, Geneva UNO office and attending a session at the UNO and making a group presentation at the Human Rights department. I am thankful to TISS for financial support for a few conferences (under such official provision for all faculty) to enable me to attend some international conferences and also to the universities and academicians who invited me with financial support. A few of my research articles were published in volumes abroad. I worked with senior academics from the USA and UK, France and Germany; I specially wish to express my gratitude to Professor Walter Allen of UCLA who invited and financed my trips and encouraged me to grow. Surprisingly, I never got an opportunity to visit the USA although I have worked and interacted with some prominent academicians from America. Somehow I feel I was recognized and appreciated more overseas than in my own country. It was not so easy to prove my worth nor was it a matter of favour but certainly it was a matter of free and unbiased academic discourse and honest appreciation unlike in Indian academic circles. On every visit abroad and over every discourse I used to remember my past, my childhood, parents and the hardships. At such times I used to get overcome with emotions.

At times I found it difficult to believe that I am the same Govardhan, friend of the classmates in village till the 7th standard who studied with me and dropped out due to some or the other reasons and have been living life in pathetic conditions. I would have been the same as them had I not persisted in my education. It has been really a very narrow and unbelievable escape. What made me survive educationally? What was the source of the spirit and motivation behind it? Can one describe it as luck? No, it was a strong super source of motivation and the spirit of Dr. B.R. Ambedkar and the enthusiasm he generated through his movement and my parents with whom I used to feel illiterate because I never could share with them my success and achievements. It can be said that my life with its shocks-after-shocks, emotional, social and cultural, that education gave me, helped me to move upwards very high.

Professionally I would call it a compulsion first and then choice. Compulsion because nothing else was possible due to several constraints and inabilities owing to background. I took on everything as a challenge added with hard work and was always open to learn and unlearn. I was fortunate to begin my professional career at the prestigious Institute and retire from the same place. I retired with an immense degree of satisfaction, although I faced several problems and odds based on social and academic grounds.

One most important thing I realized during my job is that it is too difficult to enter into academics and into a reputed institution/university and also to survive. This is because in the Indian academic world the network of established academicians belongs mostly to upper castes and particularly Brahmins. This has been the case since independence and even before. This is like the net working that is operative in the judiciary. Such people orient, train and guide their own people and hardly allow others to get in. Thanks to the reservation policy which assured me a place at least at the entry point. Secondly, I am very sure if you are good in your subject and develop abilities and show an acceptable performance, no one would dare to point at you. At the same time one must show preparedness to digest the disappointment if one is not acknowledged and recognized. But the secret is to keep trying sincerely and you can do anything.

At the same time I express my gratitude to all those who encouraged and supported me in my work. There are some people who are pragmatic in thinking and practice, who are sensitive to social issues and try and help you and support you, although sometimes from a distance and only when it is convenient. The major problem in academics I faced was that of English language. Since it is the mother language for high level of achievements, both educationally and professionally, it divides the takers into two major categories—that of the elite coming with social, cultural and language capital and the others who come from a vernacular background with poor training in English language. So English becomes a source of deprivation leading to educational inequality and hierarchy. In my case, I think whatever level I performed I could have done three times better if my English was up to the mark. It is sad that even after seven decades the policy makers and the government could not find a solution to this problem. Neither has any appropriate alternative been found nor is the training in English done properly. Effectively, the absolute majority of youths in India end up in frustration and do badly in education and thereby their talent and skills remain without nurture. This is against the value of equality of educational opportunity and a big loss to the country. Due to this language handicap, I suffered a lot. I developed an inferiority complex when I was compared with those from a convent background and at times felt discouraged and demoralized. However, I was determined to improve it by listening to speakers carefully, practising reading and writing, learning grammar, making efforts to improve pronunciation and vocabulary. I have been doing so consistently. Still I do think there is scope for further improvement. I even now do not claim to know the language perfectly. My academic vocabulary still needs improvement and more so out of academics. My son and daughter are both lucky not to have this language problem because they studied in convent schools and are much better than me. Not only this, both often help me to correct my language and do language editing for publications too. Tragically, however, both of them lost their grip over the mother tongue as I did during the course of time. Educationally, I call it a situation of crisis that leads to making youths incapable for the best academic performance to survive in the national and now global competition. The success stories in this context are insignificant in number and need thorough empirical probe.

Where There is a Will, There is a Way: As Dean of Social Protection Office

The efforts made by the TISS under the leadership of Professor Parasuraman as Director towards inclusion of the marginalized groups are noteworthy in the history of higher education institutions in the country. After he took over as Director in 2004 many activities and programmes were introduced to support education of such groups besides fully implementing the reservation policy at all levels. Both administrative and academic reshuffling took place including change in the vision and mission statements that clearly speak for the downtrodden. The mission statement was—"To be an institution of excellence in higher education that continually responds to the changing social realities through the development and application of knowledge, towards creating a people-centred and ecologically sustainable society that promotes and protects the dignity, equality, social justice and human rights for all, with special emphasis on marginalized and vulnerable groups." Prof. Parasuraman was a faculty for many years at the TISS and then joined international organizations abroad. Again he came back after a few years and joined as director. Prior to him there were three directors out of which two completed their five-year terms. However, the situation was not that good; except the implementation of the reservations mechanically, the traditionally existing elite nature of the Institute continued. Coincidentally, the position of Liaison Officer (LO) was offered to me already before Parasuraman joined. This position and its office is a mandatory device provided by the government and is very crucial and important for implementing the policy and all other related matters. It is an honorary post offered to a senior professor with separate office staff. It plays a watch dog and reports to the government at prescribed intervals. Prof. Parasuraman changed the name to Social Protection Office (SPO) and designation as Dean and scope of the office covering OBC, Minority and PWD categories in addition to original SC-ST categories. Thus, in all, a little more than half the students fall in these categories on the line of prescribed reserved seats for each category (SC 15 per cent, ST 8 per cent, OBC 27 per cent and PWD 3 per cent). Same number of reserved seats are applicable for faculty positions and the administrative staff. That means this becomes an additional responsibility for the faculty who takes it over. However, the Dean has to be really sensitive socially, aware of all provisions and rules and pragmatic in thoughts and capable of handling the office successfully.

After I took over as LO and followed by as Dean of Social Protection Office (DSPO), I took it as a challenge and as an opportunity to contribute to the cause of all deprived sections. Being an insider to the deprivation faced by these sections, I had first hand experiences of discrimination and issues concerning the reservation policy and all related matters. First of all, I took stock of backlog positions in the faculty and the admin staff and proposed for the Director to opt for a special recruitment drive to which he agreed instantly. Accordingly, whatever I used to propose within rules he used to accept and implement. In addition, there were some additional programmes proposed and implemented successfully: like pre and post-admission orientation programmes with travel reimbursement, food and accommodation facilities. A video film was produced with the help of an external professional agency on how to prepare for the entrance exam, how to face an interview, group discussion, etc besides organizing special sessions on motivation, sensitization, communication skills and confidence building. The students used to be from all over India, of both genders, with rural background, first generation learners and the majority from the vernacular medium. It was ensured that each selection panel was represented by an SC-ST-OBC member and students were allowed to speak in Hindi if not comfortable with English. This gave such satisfactory and surprising results that each year there used to be between 10 and 15 students coming from deprived backgrounds who were admitted out of the reserved category with unreserved seats. All SC-ST students whose income was below the prescribed limit were allowed to seek admission without paying fees that particular time. The government used to pay later on their behalf. Again after admission, there used to be post admission orientation and English language classes with a facility of language laboratory in the library. In addition to all this, my office was open to everyone at any time during office hours for anything they needed. Emotional, moral and social support play a pivotal role in such cases and no one knew that better than me. The success was so remarkable that every year three-four or more students from deprived backgrounds used go abroad under the exchange programme with MOUs provisions. It is so satisfying and exhilarating that all can do it, we can do it, they can do it; if given the opportunity with sincere efforts and facilities. One more very important and highly appreciative example was of a student of the MSW course in the recent past. A young married man and father of two children called Vivek (name changed) who belongs to the SC community and works as Safai Kamgar for the Mumbai Municipal Corporation and living in a 10 by 10 room provided by the municipal corporation in a *kamgar basti*. His job is to collect garbage with others from house to house in a municipal van and dispose of it at the dumping ground. Somehow he got inspired to study further and applied to TISS for a postgraduate course. He got admission but had very poor English language skills. Facing all kinds of difficulties, Vivek started studying during the day and worked during the night. Finally at the exam time he found it difficult to write in English. Restless and frustrated, he approached me as DSPO with an appeal to allow him to write the exam in Marathi. After consulting the Deputy Director and explaining his background, he was permitted to write the exam in Marathi but I had to find an evaluator. He wrote the exam and passed it. This was the first time in the TISS history that a student was allowed to write the exam in a vernacular language. Credit is due to the TISS. During his Masters, he happened to go to South Africa for a period of four months under an exchange programme. After achieving his PG (postgraduation), he applied for MPhil/PhD integratedd course and was admitted there as well. Being entitled, Vivek applied for study leave in his office. His immediate boss and the highest authority in the corporation bluntly refused to consider his case saying that there was no such provision for safai kamgars. This went on for a few months. Somehow the matter drew the attention of the print media. Thanks to a lady reporter of *The Indian Express* in Mumbai. She did detailed reporting of the case and brought the matter to the national level. The then Prime Minister Dr. Manmohan Singh paid attention and ordered to sanction him the leave immediately. So he completed his MPhil and is now pursuing a doctorate. This speaks of many things when it comes to the downtrodden, poor and their struggle to come out of the traditional social stigma and use education as a means (the only viable means available) to achieve educational, occupational, economic and finally, social mobility. Tomorrow he would be labelled as an SC elite and targeted in many ways accused of misusing the reservations and attributed it to change in the caste system. I wonder how and who really would be willing to face all that to reach that level. Sociology in India is basically missing out in recording and analysing such basic and harsh social realities. Is it because of bias or complete insensitivity or out of priority areas? Vivek is now a PhD scholar and aiming to be on the Safai Kamgar Commission, Government of India. I wish him luck.

As Dean of the School of Education

After major academic restructuring, the unit for Child and Youth Studies was dissolved. The major change was to establish schools and each department and unit came under respective schools. The School of Education was a new creation with two new centres under that: Centre for Elementary Education Studies and Centre for Higher Education. The Unit for Sociology of Education was merged into this school with its office in the new campus. Nandini Manjrekar, Disha Nawani, Sthabir Khora and myself moved to the school, whereas Padma Sarangpani started functiong from Bengaluru. Padma Velaskar, Ranu Jain and Leena Abraham did not join us but continued with the Centre for Studies in Sociology of Education, although we waited for long for them. I think it was more an issue of internal politics with the director. I was Dean of the School of Education and Chairman of the Centre for Higher Education. So I held two dean positions, one of the social protection office and another of the school and chairing the one-man Centre for Higher Education till my retirement. What a unique situation. Vacant positions and additional positions that were due for recruitment are yet to be filled for many reasons including that of UGC functioning.

I am fully satisfied and convinced that all my responsibilities at both deans' offices were fulfilled with great enthusiasm and care to the best of my experiences and abilities.

7

What Next?

LOOKING BACK, LOOKING FORWARD

Overall Experiences

Overall experiences have been a mixture of good and bad for me, both at academic, administrative and social levels. Good because no one ever interfered or questioned my academic activities and responsibilities; be it research projects, teaching course, joining various committees at national level or visits abroad or organizing national and international seminars. At times there used to be administrative issues that bothered me, probably because of perceptions and attitude towards me being a strict person with a non-compromising approach or due to my social identity. Everyone used to be conscious while talking or interacting with me more because of my position as DSPO. But right through, I was confined to this office only and a strong identity was built only on and around SC-ST-OBC issues while all my academic contributions were ignored. No one looked at me beyond administration. I always felt a professional distance with all, including my colleagues, in the school. However, I must admit that I enjoyed the academic freedom the most, which generally is not found in the universities in India.

Regarding the students and staff belonging to the same

community, there was a sense of unity and cohesiveness as when some issue used to come up but overall I used to feel a distance with them too. This could be because of my nature and difference in approach in resolving the issues. Although I have been outspoken, I used to be taken for granted most of the time. I never expected favours from any student or staff. Sometimes I was expected to do an undue favour since I shared the same social background. I always bluntly refused to do it and hence received a lot of criticism and blame. However, I hardly felt close to them and was never helped and supported during any kind of personal, professional or social problems. Thus I was not a group member for both the SC-ST and the general community in the institution. There were times when I used to feel isolated but never expressed it. This, exactly has been the situation in society in general right through my life and professional career. I am grateful to those few, who respected me and appreciated my work and efforts, however covertly. I am compelled to mention my expectations from people in general and from my own community people in particular that we need to change our approach, must be prepared with knowledge and social skills, work very hard, be highly critical and analytical and then face everything. This will leave no scope for untoward criticism or for putting us down socially and morally. We must always introspect, find out weaknesses and improve them. I would like to emphasize with due apologies, that this is not an advice but a simple and basic expectation from all my educated brothers and sisters.

The Educated Elites

It is generally believed that those educated and upwardly mobile SCs only enjoy all the benefits and forget their own people. It is not true that only the educated elite enjoy the benefits at the cost of common people. Even at this juncture a majority of educated and well settled people belong to the first generation and, invariably their achievements are based on struggles of all kinds. They faced all odds including deprivation and discrimination during education and were always compelled to carry the stigma of being incapable. However, they are few in number and always struggling to settle down, at family level, community level and society in general. The mindset is constantly sandwiched between the self and other elite. Generally people look at their job positions and sound economic status for which they get targeted. But their struggle, diligence, motivation and inspirations are conveniently ignored. They also suffer from anxiety and identity crisis and find themselves caught between traditonal stigmatized and modern secular identity. Our education system is such that it alienates us from our own roots, culture and community. Self isolation is the end result of the social and economic structure that necessarily runs through higher education; the only available means for them. The circumstances make them feel and live like that. Of course, there are some exceptions but they exist in all societies and communities. However, the gap between the educated and common people is widening within their own community. This always leads to a dichotomy between 'we' and 'they'. Do the 'they' ever make real efforts to know the issue, come closer without bias and have real social intercourse? The social intercourse appears to be there but it is superficial with visible contradictions between public and private life, at macro and micro levels.

The Social and Political Movements

Social movement among Dalits after Dr. Ambedkar has been weakening every day. This is mainly because after Ambedkar, his leadership in the social field and social activism has been poor because it mainly depended on petty and symbolic issues with emotional approach and lacking skills. There has always been the mix up of social issues with political issues and it is mainly confined to a particular section of the community known as Buddhists (ex-Mahars) while all the other major communities have remained out of purview of the activism. The same things happened with the political movement: leadership got divided into several fractions with individualism. There has been a thorough communication gap between the masses and the leadership. Also one can observe lack of political and ideological maturity that has led to isolation from other liberal and progressive parties in the country to the extent that it is next to impossible to get even one MP (Member of Parliament) elected on its own. I am sure the leadership among the Dalits has always kept the educated elite away for reasons best known to them. In turn this has led to a great loss with severe crisis in social and political discourses of the Dalits. Although it gave great hopes at the beginning, the Dalit Panther movement emerged as a result of a failure in political leadership. However, it also got into a similar situation like the (RPI) Republican Party of India. One of the important causes for such a situation has been that the ruling party has always been successful in using the leadership for its gains by dividing the leaders and secondly it has been due to lack of proper training and orientation to the leadership and the second circle of leaders. Another important area of failure has been the religion, i.e. Buddhism, prescribed by Dr. Ambedkar. It remained mainly within the Mahars. No one bothered to spread it to the Matangs and Chambhars and other castes, although it has been open to everyone. This is not to say that there are no achievements at all. There are many successes on many fronts. Given the long history of the suppression and ignorance, it is probably too early to expect that quality of strong and staunch movements and leadership against facing all odds.

Educational Situation: A Matter of Real Worry

As rightly pronounced and propagated by Ambedkar, education is the key for emancipation for all the downtrodden. He meant modern education, unlike not the traditional one which is not secular and open to all. His efforts were immense in bringing education to the forefront of his movement; also by actually supporting and encouraging higher education of some Dalits to study abroad with financial support from the government. Availability of the National Overseas Scholarship scheme for SC-ST, post Matric Scholarships, freeship and hostel facilities are the major achievements of his struggle. Education was the major agenda of his movement via the Samta Sainik Dal that was practically working hard to make aware and motivate people for their children's education. I am certainly a product of such efforts of the SSD. However, after his death the education movement slowly weakened. Today education has become a source of money making which is difficult to access and afford. The quality of education is decided on the basis of the fluency of the English language and Western sophistication. Higher education turned out to be urban biased, expensive, language (English) and gender biased. Dalits have had to face multiple problems to access education, and continue to do so while getting educated and even after it. They constantly and consistently face issues including deprivation, humiliation and discrimination. Educational survival ratio till higher education is very poor. The higher they reach in the education level, the more discrimination they face. This may happen because they become aware and conscious of the realities and causes behind it. Above all, English as a medium of instruction proves to be a monster for most Indians; and more so for Dalits as it deprives them of good quality teaching at nationally reputed colleges and universities. Wastage and stagnation are major issues in their educational journey. It is a pity that the government has been unable to decide on its language policy for education. Educational policy and planning has been biased in favour of a few upper and middle class/caste with the last priority given for the downtrodden. Efforts to achieve policy goals and implementation of programmes/schemes has been very poor, perhaps due to bureaucratic problems and biases in the minds of officials who generally belong to the upper castes. Today, our education system is such that it produces misfits for family, community and our nation. Indeed, it is high time to answer these questions: Education for what, for whom and by whom? Globalization and privatization of education have rubbed salt into the wound.

As a teacher, I could see the difference in what education was till 1990, the landmark year of globalization and information technology, and now in the 21st century in the country in terms of its quality, employability, knowledge generation and skills that higher education imparts. At the same time perceptions and approach to education got shifted from nobility to commodity. The same is the case with students that they go with short cuts and casual approach to everything. Dalits are caught in between. They can neither afford an expensive private English-language education, nor can they access easily the government-funded education. God knows what will be the future of education in India and the future of all the poor who struggle to access it.

Reservation Policy: Honey Drop on the Tip of the Finger

Reservation policy in India has been a most controversial issue unlike any other country. Let us first learn that the policy is widely known as Affirmative Action Policy across the world and is adopted by the majority of countries including China, USA, Japan, and it even existed in the former USSR. The names of other countries that follow the policy are: New Zealand (with a fixed quota of reserved seats like India), Pakistan, Australia, South America and African countries. Each country decided the base to adopt the policy (also known as preferential treatment) such as, race, ethnicity, religion and language depending on social composition of that society. In India it is based on caste which is its basic social reality. It may please be noted that no country has adopted the policy based on poverty or class. So the policy in India is based on caste(s) that are socially and educationally backward due to social and historical reasons and adopted more as compensation for centuries old sufferings with the noble and democratic principle of social justice. Historically, during the late 19th and early 20th centuries, the progressive princely states like Kolhapur, Baroda, Travancore and Mysore introduced the reservation policy and other welfare programmes for the depressed classes. It is through consistent efforts that the policy was adopted for SCs in 1933 and STs in 1958, eventually becoming a Constitutional Commitment. The initiative started by Jyotirao Phule was taken forward to fruition by Dr. B.R. Ambedkar. However, the origin with constitutional recognition of the policy is in the Poona Pact of 1933 between Gandhi and Ambedkar as a solution to Gandhi's act of fast unto death over the granting of dual constituency for SCs. Dr. Ambedkar after signing the Pact said that it was his first and the last defeat in his social-political movement. However, there has been a great mistake and misunderstanding among the elite and masses about the time period of the policy. It is clearly mentioned that only the political reservations would be for ten years and there is no mention of educational and employment reservations and would depend on how it is implemented and what the achievements are. The entire issue unfortunately got politicized, implemented in a haphazard way with no real will behind it and therefore is renewed and continued merely for political benefits.

Reservation Policy Controversy

First of all, I must admit and express my sincere thanks to the policy that provided me with opportunities in my entire educational and employment career. Without which it would have been next to impossible for me to achieve what I have achieved. And I am sure this is true of all those who have earned education and positions in their lives, though not easily. However perceptions of people are just the opposite; as if reservations go with birth in one's life and once you avail them, everything is readily available. No, it is never the case; there are prescribed criteria and conditions to avail the reservation and other facilities. For example, firstly one needs to procure a caste certificate to prove one's caste and to procure it there are several hurdles including bribing; there are grossly missing mechanisms to make them capable of availing these provisions. It is not enough to make the opportunity available, it is equally necessary to provide support and the environment to enable and avail of those opportunities appropriately and aptly. Despite this, a significant number of people have benefited although in a limited manner. It was next to impossible to access education and get into white collar modern jobs for these sections in such a biased and unequal situation otherwise. The public opinion seems to be against the policy which is more out of biases, ignorance and lack of sensitivity. There are social and political lobbies working against the policy and creating public opinion against it. I would rather argue that if one withdraws the policy, what will be the viable alternative and who and which government will ensure education, employment, health and dignity to all those who have been treated like animals for centuries? Who will actually be benefited if the base is shifted from caste to class? Now the counter argument is that why only oppose the reservations in isolation? Why not question the traditional inherited ownership and monopoly over material property like land, gold, trade, money and non-material property like cultural and social power, education and knowledge and the ultimate power that has been enjoyed throughout? I am sure it is out of logic and reasoning to target the policy and its critics are biased with such a narrow mind even in the days of modern and democratic values. It is indeed a fact that the reservation policy has been reduced to a stigma for such people who are being equated with being undeserving, and are a source of hampering quality. Now who will decide quality and merit? In the absence of dignity of labour and work culture, is it that these people are responsible for such a pathetic situation in politics, business, education and administration added to corruption and favouritism? Ultimately it is the caste that matters in public life and private life, in marriage and love, in residence, in office and politics, in authority and power, in education and knowledge, in media and culture and in language. I wonder why and how Germany could do so well as compared to India when Germany and India began with the same timeline; despite the fact that Germany was totally broken during the Second World War.

However, at the same time the benefits of the policy and the other provisions could not reach all the castes among SCs across the country. It is believed that a particular caste(s) among them in a particular state has been taking away all the benefits; like Buddhists(former Mahars) of Maharashtra, Jatavas of Uttar Pradesh and Malas-Madigas of Andhra Pradesh and so on. In reality, the SCs are an equally heterogeneous community socially and have social hierarchy among them. Those castes that are population-wise large and have given up traditional occupation and follow Dr. Ambedkar have done much better as compared to others. At the same time, there are as many as 1092 officially recognized SCs in the country with diverse backgrounds and all of them have been treated as a single social entity. So the planning, policy and the programmes for their development proved unsuitable and inadequate in many ways. It is not they who are responsible, rather the approach has been wrong. The real benefits of the policy are at the higher level of education. It is very difficult to reach the higher level of education due to several reasons and very few are sustained. One has to have a minimum of an undergraduate level degree to get a high profile public sector job. Despite all this, there we find a high level of educated unemployment or under employment among these communities. This is added by privatization and IT issues in recent times. The second generation is badly affected educationally and employment-wise.

Paradoxically, the demand for reservations is increasing over a period of time. This demand has more of a political coverage than is actually needed. Castes like Jats, Patels, Gurjars and Marathas are demanding reservation on the basis of their economic backwardness. Undoubtedly there are poor sections in each caste and community and the government must be committed to ensure education and employment for the really needy first and there is no need to question their demands. But if one looks back in the past and the present of such castes, one finds that these are the very communities that have been dominant and enjoying power and authority in social and political spheres. They have generally been at the front of exploitation and suppression of the lower castes and the SC-ST. Will the reservation policy neutralize the situation socially and culturally? In all, the issue of reservation policy got narrowed down to a political gimmick and the noble principle of justice and equality got defeated due to the casual approach of the government, politicians and intellectuals. We must be the best example in the world for apathy and pretentions towards issues like these.

Privatization and the Marginalized

Globalization and government policies have led to privatization of education and public organizations and hence the SCs-STs and OBCs get further deprived in many ways in the situation where knowledge and skills are in great demand. Yes, globalization has increased the opportunities, but only for the affluent middle class and upper castes and English-speaking elite who are insignificant in number and still monopolizing all the opportunities due to social networking and traditional social and economic comfort. This is known as the neo-caste in modern global discourse. The gradual withdrawal from education and employment has a direct negative impact on these communities as there is no reservation policy applicable in the private sector. Reservation policy in the private sector Bill was introduced in parliament but is still pending, as it was opposed in parliament due to the strong corporate lobby and right wing politics. This is reflective of their mindset with regard to the policy. I am sure all those who oppose the policy are under the impression that the policy is at the cost of quality and those who avail it are undeserving and incapable. This is not true at all, rather it is highly biased and stereotypical. In fact, these people have immense potential with their strong emotional, physical and intellectual strength in addition to their hardy and tough life. Their qualities have always remained without proper nourishment. It is a matter of one's approach and sensitivity towards the issue. I am sure if the proper environment and training are provided they will perform on par with anyone. There are several examples of best performance in every field. I often feel surprised when I listen to adverse remarks and criticism in un-Parliamentary language from even educated persons over the policy and its potential beneficiaries. I can only pity them. I think it is not the matter of givers and takers rather it is the matter of due legitimate share. Everyone seems to be talking negatively against the policy but no one takes responsibility to initiate practical training, orientation and skill development initiatives as social responsibility; it is as if the people from these sections of our society are not deserving. It may be noted that no research study or report provides the evidence that the reservations lead to lowring the quality or affects work performance or effiency.

LOOKING INTO SELF

I began with very little and retired with full academic and professional achievements and satisfaction that has been due to educational upward mobility that led to occupational, economic and social mobility—not without perseverance and struggle to survive and to succeed. My entire life journey makes me look into the self and reminds me of the strengths and weaknesses, ups and downs, highs and lows, encouragement and discouragements and the support of really sensitive persons. The high spirit and motivation received from Babasaheb Ambedkar and both my families—parental and marital have been invaluable. However, my educational survival must be taken as exceptional as it was next to impossible in the given social and economic situations caused due to inherent social and religious sanctions. Poverty, caste, untouchabilty, discrimination always chased me and pushed me towards an inferiority complex and weakend confidence. The village, the towns, the cities and the countries gave me different exposure. At the same time, this reminds me of the limitations of the forces of change, i.e. urban life, education, profession, reservations, etc. Do they really lead to complete modern and secular life? I say no! These two are caught between the traditional and the modern, western versus eastern as long as the individual behind these operating forces are governed by basic social institutions like religion, caste, community, family, etc. It is a process of continuity and change. Continuity is seen to be within and change is from outside. In the Indian society today the priorities have changed both at individual and societal level. Caste, poverty, untouchabilty and exploitation have occupied the last row. Social reform is silent. The policy of reservations gets politicized which has led to us forgetting its basic objectives and the takers of the policy get further drawn into stigma and need.

I am the first generation product of the movement initiated by Dr. Babasaheb Ambedkar and as is the case with the first line, I had to face problems at many levels with great intensity. However, even if the intensity of such problems has weakened to a great extent it continues to exist in new forms. Awareness, access and affordability got restricted to a very few, whereas the majority continues to be out of discourse. This differs from generation to generation and caste to caste among all the communities in general and among the Dalits in particular. But the issue of identity crisis became stronger when everyone started taking pride in their own caste (s). Do we need to relearn the Sociology of India? This needs to be anwered after understanding the different challenges, expectations and hopes for the future of the Dalit youth.

With many salutes to Dr. Bhimrao Ramji Amedkar, the great saviour!